MW01206489

# Society Of Colonial Wars In The State Of Wisconsin

Society of Colonial Wars.

THE

# SOCIETY OF
# COLONIAL WARS

IN THE

STATE OF WISCONSIN

LIST OF OFFICERS AND MEMBERS

INCLUDING PEDIGREES AND A RECORD OF THE SERVICES
PERFORMED BY ANCESTORS IN THE WARS
OF THE COLONIES

Milwaukee
Printed for the Society by
.Burdick & Allen
1906

ELLIS BAKER USHER,
HENRY ALVIN CROSBY,
WILLIAM WARD WIGHT,
Committee on Publication.

# Official Roll

# Officers and Gentlemen of the Council

1905

Governor
## WYMAN KNEELAND FLINT

Deputy Governor
## CHARLES GAGER STARK

Lieutenant Governor
## THOMAS LATHROP KENNAN

Secretary
## ALBERT KELLOGG STEBBINS

Deputy Secretary
## HARRY LAFAYETTE KELLOGG

Treasurer
## JONATHAN FRANKLIN PEIRCE

Registrar
## *HAROLD GREEN UNDERWOOD

Chancelor
## WILLIAM WARD WIGHT

Genealogist
## CHARLES COPELAND RUSSELL

Historian
## ELLIS BAKER USHER

ased

Surgeon

## NELSON ALONZO PENNOYER

Chaplain

## Rev. HORATIO GATES

Deputy Governor General

## WILLIAM WOLCOTT STRONG

Gentlemen of the Council

## WILLIAM HENRY UPHAM
## HOWARD GREENE
## OLIVER FREDERIC DWIGHT
## WILLIAM STARK SMITH
## GERRY WHITING HAZLETON

Governor

COL. WILLIAM WOLCOTT STRONG, 1897-1903
WYMAN KNEELAND FLINT, 1904-1905

Deputy Governor

FRANK SLOSSON, 1897
WYMAN KNEELAND FLINT, 1898
HN WILLIAM PETERSON LOMBARD, 1899, 1901-1903
ARTHUR NYE McGEOCH, 1900
WILLIAM WOLCOTT STRONG, 1904
CHARLES GAGER STARK, 1905

Lieutenant Governor

CAPTAIN PHILIP READE, U. S. A., 1897
WILLIAM JAMES STARR, 1898-1903
CHARLES GAGER STARK, 1904
THOMAS LATHROP KENNAN, 1905

1898

Delegates to the General Court

WILLIAM WOLCOTT STRONG

WYMAN KNEELAND FLINT

JOHN WILLIAM PETERSON LOMBARD

CHARLES GAGER STARK

WILLIAM KING COFFIN


Alternates

FRANK SLOSSON

WILLIAM HENRY UPHAM

ELLIS BAKER USHER

WILLIAM WARD WIGHT

WILLIAM JAMES STARR


1902

Delegates to the General Court

WILLIAM WOLCOTT STRONG

HOWARD GREENE

FRANK GORDON BIGELOW

JOHN WILLIAM PETERSON LOMBARD

ELLIS BAKER USHER


Alternates

CHARLES HERMAN RUGGLES

FRANCIS JEWETT JOHNSON

*HAROLD GREEN UNDERWOOD

WILLIAM HENRY UPHAM

CHARLES GAGER STARK

*Deceased

1905

Delegates to the General Court

WYMAN KNEELAND FLINT

WILLIAM KING COFFIN

*HAROLD GREEN UNDERWOOD

JONATHAN FRANKLIN PEIRCE

JOHN WYMAN FLINT

Alternates

COL. PHILIP READE, U. S. A.

ALBERT KELLOGG STEBBINS

WILLIAM STARK SMITH

OLIVER CLYDE FULLER

FRANCIS GARDINER FLINT

*Deceased

# Historical

ON April 26, 1897, a meeting was held in Kenosha, Wis., for the purpose of organizing a Society of Colonial Wars in the State of Wisconsin. At this meeting a letter was read from the Secretary General of the General Society of Colonial Wars, authorizing the formation of a Society of Colonial Wars in this state, and acting upon that authority a preliminary organization was effected and the Constitution of the Society of Colonial Wars in the State of Massachusetts, with one or two changes, was temporarily adopted, and officers were elected to serve until the first General Court.

On July 28, 1897, the first Special Court of the Society was held in Milwaukee and Articles of Incorporation were signed, all the officers being re-elected to serve until the date of the first General Court mentioned in the Articles of Incorporation.

At a meeting of the Council held in Milwaukee on October 26, 1897, the By-Laws of the Society were adopted.

The first General Court of the Society was held on December 22, 1897, when officers for the ensuing year were elected. Immediately after the adjournment of the Court, the first annual dinner of the Society was held at Hotel Pfister, ten members being present and four guests of the Society.

At a meeting of the Council held January 14, 1898, it was unanimously voted to publish the first Year Book of the Society.

The History of the Society of Colonial Wars in the State

of Wisconsin is brief, but shows a steady growth and interest in patriotic research.

November 15, 1899. Resignation of William Lyman Mason, on account of permanent removal to Washington, was presented to Council and accepted.

December 21, 1899. The annual Court of the Society of Colonial Wars in the State of Wisconsin was convened at the Hotel Pfister, Milwaukee, and officers elected for the ensuing year.

November 7, 1901. Application of Mr. Paul Denison Sexton, now living in Chicago, to be transferred from the Wisconsin to the Illinois Society, granted.

December 21, 1901. Annual Court of the Society of Colonial Wars was held at the Milwaukee Club. Officers were elected for the ensuing year. On motion of Mr. Payne $25.00 was appropriated to the McKinley Memorial Association. On motion of Mr. Camp the Governor appointed a committee to consider the advisability of requesting the co-operation of Societies of the state to endeavor to assist in the passage of a bill before Congress for the erecting of a memorial to President Abraham Lincoln.

April 30, 1902. Howard Greene tendered his resignation as secretary. Resignation was accepted, to take effect upon the election of his successor. William Stevens Brockway was elected to fill the unexpired term as secretary.

December 20, 1902. The annual Court of the Society of Colonial Wars in the State of Wisconsin, was convened at the Milwaukee Club, Milwaukee. The following resolution was unanimously adopted:

Resolved, that Article IV of the Articles of Incorporation of the Society of Colonial Wars in the State of Wisconsin be, and they are hereby, amended by striking out the word "three" where it occurs in the fifth line of said article, as the same appears in the records of the Secretary of the Society; and inserting in place thereof the word "five"; so that said article when so amended shall read:

IV. "The general officers of such corporation shall be a governor, a deputy governor, a lieutenant governor, a secretary, a deputy secretary, a treasurer, a registrar, a historian, a genealogist, a chaplain, a chancelor, and a surgeon. Such officers with five other members of this corporation to be elected like them, annually, shall constitute the council, which shall manage the affairs of the corporation."

Officers were elected for the ensuing year.

The regular annual banquet followed the business meeting. The speakers were: Hon. Gerry W. Hazleton, Hon. George W. Peck, Capt. F. B. McCoy, Judge L. H. Bancroft and Harold G. Underwood.

December 21, 1903. The annual Court of the Society of Colonial Wars in the State of Wisconsin was convened at the Milwaukee Club, Milwaukee. Officers were elected for the ensuing year. The regular annual banquet followed the business meeting. Nineteen were present. Guests: Major L. W. Cooke, Captain David A. Hall; General Charles King and Captain A. B. Davis sent regrets.

January 13, 1904. Resolutions of sorrow adopted, relative to death of Bedford Brown Hopkins, copies of which were sent to the family of the deceased.

The Society gave $50 to the George Rogers Clark Society Children of the American Revolution for a bust to be placed in the Public Library.

October 9, 1904. The Society sent a delegation to attend

funeral services of Henry Clay Payne, Deputy Governor General for Wisconsin, and afterwards adopted resolutions.

December 21, 1904.   General Court and annual dinner held at Milwaukee Club.

A resolution ·was introduced authorizing the preparation of a new lineage book for the Society; the resolution was adopted and upon motion the Governor appointed Ellis Baker Usher, Henry Alvin Crosby and William Ward Wight as a Committee on Publication.

At this Court the Historian's report was in the nature of a sketch of the life of Deputy Governor General Henry Clay Payne.

At the dinner the speakers of the evening were Rev. H. H. Jacobs, Col. L. W. Cooke, U. S. A., Lieut. W. E. V. Jacobs, R. C. S., and the Chancelor of this Society, William Ward Wight.

May 14, 1905.   A meeting of the Council was held to take formal action with reference to the death of Harold Green Underwood, a charter member and the Registrar of this Society.

December 20, 1905.   General Court and annual dinner held at the Plankinton House.   Principal speaker, Capt. William V. Judson, U. S. A.

# Articles of Incorporation

THE undersigned, being adult persons and residents of the State of Wisconsin, and being desirous to form a corporation under Chapter 66 of the Revised Statutes of Wisconsin and of the laws amendatory thereof, do make, sign and acknowledge written articles as follows:

## I.

They declare that they associate for the purpose of forming a corporation under said revised Statutes, and that the purposes thereof are to cultivate and advance literature and art and to foster and promote patriotism, by collecting and preserving manuscripts, rolls, relics and records pertaining to the history of the American Colonies; by providing suitable commemorations, or memorials, and by preparing historical papers relating to the American Colonial period; by perpetuating the names and services of those who, in military, naval and civil positions of high trust and responsibility, assisted in the establishment, defense, and preservation of the American Colonies; by inspiring in the members of this corporation the fraternal and patriotic spirit of the colonists and by increasing in the community respect and reverence for those whose public services made the freedom and unity of the United States possible.

## II.

The name of such corporation shall be SOCIETY OF COLONIAL WARS IN THE STATE OF WISCONSIN. Its location shall be the City of Milwaukee, in the County of Milwaukee, in said State.

## III.

This corporation is organized without capital stock and exclusively for benevolent purposes, and no dividends or pecuniary profits shall ever be made or declared by such corporation to its members.

## IV.

The general officers of such corporation shall be a Governor, a Deputy Governor, a Lieutenant Governor, a Secretary, a Deputy Secretary, a Treasurer, a Registrar, a Historian, a Genealogist, a Chaplain, a Chancelor and a Surgeon. Such officers with five other members of this corporation to be elected like them, annually, shall constitute the Council, which shall manage the affairs of the corporation.

## V.

The principal duties of the general officers shall be: The Governor, or in the case of his absence or other disqualification, the Deputy Governor or the Lieutenant Governor, shall preside at all meetings of the corporation and of the council. The Secretary, or in case of his absence, or other disqualification the Deputy Secretary, shall keep the records, conduct the correspondence and preserve the seal and the historical documents of the corporation.

The Treasurer shall collect and preserve the moneys of the corporation, lawfully disburse the same, and keep a true account of his receipts and expenditures.

The Registrar shall receive and preserve proofs of membership and other like documents.

The Historian shall keep a complete and detailed record of historical and commemorative celebrations of the corporation, edit such documents as the corporation shall publish, and prepare annually a necrology and biographies of deceased members.

The Genealogist shall investigate and pass upon all applications for membership.

The Chancelor shall pass upon all questions of a legal character affecting the corporation. All the principal officers shall perform such other duties as the By-Laws shall impose and such as appertain to their several offices respectively in like corporations.

The Council shall devise and procure a seal, prepare, amend and repeal By-Laws, provide and prescribe the duties of committees, fix the quorum of the council and of the corporation (which may be less than one-half of either body) and perform such other duties as the By-Laws may prescribe, such as appertain to such a body in like corporations and such as are necessary to carry out the purposes of the organization.

## VI.

The following named persons:

> William Wolcott Strong,
> Frank Slosson,
> Philip Reade,
> William Henry Upham,
> Wyman Kneeland Flint,
> William Ward Wight,
> Ellis Baker Usher,
> William Chester Swain,
> James Kneeland,
> William King Coffin,
> John William Peterson Lombard,
> Grant Fitch,
> Charles Curtis Brown,
> Nelson Alonzo Pennoyer,
> William Lyman Mason,
> Herbert Wight Underwood,
> John Wyman Flint,
> Samuel Sweet Simmons,

and such other persons as from time to time shall be elected to membership therein by ballot in accordance with the conditions and requirements of the By-Laws, shall be the and the only members of this corporation.

## VII.

The first meeting of this corporation for the election of officers shall be held at No. 272 Martin Street, in the said city of Milwaukee, at eight o'clock in the evening of the 28th day of July, 1897. The By-Laws shall make provision for the annual meeting and for other meetings, regular and special, both of the corporation and of the council.

Witness the hands and seals of the signers hereof this 10th day of July, 1897.

Signed:    WILLIAM WOLCOTT STRONG, (Seal.)
WILLIAM CHESTER SWAIN, (Seal.)
WYMAN KNEELAND FLINT, (Seal.)
WILLIAM WARD WIGHT, (Seal.)

In presence of
Signed:    FRANCES FLINT,
JENNIE L. FLINT.

# By-Laws

## SOCIETY OF COLONIAL WARS IN THE STATE OF WISCONSIN.

### ARTICLE I.

#### Of Designations

The articles of association of the Society of Colonial Wars in the State of Wisconsin may be designated herein as the Constitution of the said Society; the annual meeting of its members, as the General Court, and Special meetings as Special Courts.

### ARTICLE II.

#### Of Qualifications for Membership

Any male person of 21 years of age and above, of good moral character and reputation, shall be eligible to membership in the Society of Colonial Wars in the State of Wisconsin, who is lineally descended in the male or female line from an ancestor;

(1) Who served as a military or naval officer, or as a soldier, sailor or marine, or as a privateersman under the authority of the Colonies which afterward formed the United States, or in the forces of Great Britain which participated with those of the said colonies in any wars in which the said colonies were engaged or in which they enrolled men, from the settlement of Jamestown, May 13, 1607, to the battle of Lexington, April 19, 1775.

(2)    Who held office in any of the Colonies between the dates above mentioned, either as;

(a)    Director General or Vice Director General in the Colony of New Netherlands.

(b)    Governor, Lieutenant or Deputy Governor, or Lord Proprietor in the Colonies of New York, New Jersey, Virginia, Pennsylvania and Delaware.

(c)    Lord Proprietor, Governor or Deputy Governor, in Maryland or the Carolinas.

(d)    Governor, Deputy Governor or Governor's Assistant, in any of the New England Colonies.

## ARTICLE III.

### Of Initiation Fees and Dues

The Initiation Fee shall be $5.00; the Annual Dues, $5.00, payable at the General Court of each year.

The payment at any one time of $50.00 shall exempt the members so paying, from annual dues; or the payment at any one time, by a charter member, of $25.00 shall exempt the said charter member from paying annual dues.

## ARTICLE IV.

### Of Admission of Members

Every application for membership shall be made in writing, on duplicate blanks furnished by the Secretary, subscribed and sworn to by the Applicant and approved by two members of the Society over their signatures.

Applications shall be accompanied by proofs of eligibility, and such applications and proofs shall be referred to the committee on membership, which shall carefully investigate the same and report as early as may be, its recommendation thereon.

Applicants shall be elected by a Council of the Society, duly called, but a negative vote of one in five of the ballots cast, shall cause the rejection of such applicant.

Payment of the initiation fees and dues shall be a prerequisite of membership.   All elections to membership are subject to the approval of the National Society of Colonial Wars.

## ARTICLE V.

### Of the Declaration

The application of every applicant for membership shall contain, or be accompanied by, his declaration that he has not failed of admission in any other State Society of Colonial Wars and that he will use his best efforts to promote the purposes of this Society and will observe its Constitution and By-Laws.

## ARTICLE VI.

### Of Election of Officers

The officers and members of the Council and the Committee on Membership shall be elected by ballot at the General Court.

A plurality of the votes cast shall determine the choice for each officer and member of the Council, and such officers and members, together with the members of the committee on membership, shall hold office for a period of one year or until their successors shall be duly elected and qualified.

## ARTICLE VII.

### Of the Governor

The Governor, or in his absence, the Deputy Governor or Lieutenant Governor, shall preside at all Courts of the Society, under Parliamentary rules, subject to an appeal to the Society.

The Governor shall be ex-officio a member of all committees

except the nominating committee and the committee on membership.  He shall have power to convene the Council at his discretion and shall so convene it upon written request of two members of the Council or upon like request of five members of the
Society.

## ARTICLE VIII.

### Of the Secretary

The Secretary, or in case of his absence, the Deputy Secretary, shall keep a record of all meetings of the Society, and have
charge of the Seal and Certificates of Incorporation of the
Society, and documents other than those required to be otherwise deposited, and shall affix the seal to all properly authenti-
cated certificates of membership, and transmit the same to the
members to whom they may be issued.  He shall notify the
Registrar of all admissions to membership.  He shall certify all
acts of the Society, and when required, authenticate them under
seal.  He shall have charge of printing the publications issued
by the Society.  He shall incorporate in notices of the Council
meetings the names of all applicants for membership to be voted
on at that Council.  He shall give notice to each officer, who
may be affected by them, of all votes, resolutions and proceedings of the Society or of the Council, and at the General Court
or oftener, shall report the names of those candidates who have
been accepted and those who have been expelled for cause.

## ARTICLE IX.

### Of the Treasurer

The Treasurer shall deposit the funds of the Society in some
bank in the State of Wisconsin, which shall be designated by the
Council, to the credit of the Society of Colonial Wars in the
State of Wisconsin, and such funds shall be drawn thence on

the checks of the Treasurer for the purposes of the Society only. He shall render a report of his receipts and expenditures at the General Court, and oftener, if required by the Council or by the General Court.

## ARTICLE X.

### Of the Registrar

The Registrar shall receive from the Secretary and file all proofs upon which membership shall have been granted, with a list of all diplomas countersigned by him. He shall also file all documents relating to memberships which the Society may obtain, and under direction of the Council shall make copies of such papers as the owners may not be willing to leave in the permanent keeping of the Society.

## ARTICLE XI.

### Of the Genealogist and of the Historian

The Genealogist shall investigate and pass upon all applications for membership and all supplemental applications, and shall report the result of his investigations to the committee on membership.

The duties of the Historian are sufficiently set forth in the Constitution.

## ARTICLE XII.

### Of the Chaplain

The Chaplain shall be an ordained minister of a Christian Church and it shall be his duty to officiate when called upon by the Governor.

## ARTICLE XIII.

### Of the Chancelor and of the Surgeon

The Chancelor shall be a lawyer duly admitted to the bar, and it shall be his duty to give legal opinions on matters affecting the Society when called upon by the proper officers.

The Surgeon shall be a practising physician.

## ARTICLE XIV.

### Of the Council

The Council shall have the power to call Special Courts of the Society and to arrange for celebrations by the Society. It shall control and manage the affairs and funds of the Society, but shall at no time be required to take action or contract any debts for which its members shall be personally liable.

Five members of the Council shall be a quorum for the transaction of business. It shall submit to the General Court a report of its proceedings for the year then closing. It shall have the power to drop from the roll of membership the name of any member who shall be at least two years in arrears, on account of dues or other assessments, and shall fail, on proper notice being given, to pay the same within 60 days. Any member dropped, may be restored to membership at any time by the Council upon a written application, and the payment of all the arrears to the date of such application.

## ARTICLE XV.

### Of the Committee on Membership

The Committee on Membership shall consist of three members, one of whom shall be the Genealogist. Two members

shall constitute a quorum, and a negative vote of one member
shall cause an adverse report to the Council on the Candidate's
application.

The proceedings of the Committee shall be secret and con-
fidential, and the applicant who shall have been rejected by the
Council shall be ineligible for membership for the space of one
year from the date of rejection, except upon a unanimous vote
of the Committee.

## ARTICLE XVI.

### Of Vacancies and Terms of Office

The Council shall have power to appoint a member of the
Society to any office or to membership in the Council pro-
tempore, to fill a vacancy which the Society shall not have filled
by an election; provided, however, that the office of Governor
shall not be so filled by the Council, when there shall be a Deputy
Governor or a Lieutenant Governor to enter on the duties.
Should any member of the Council, other than an officer, be
absent from three consecutive Councils, his place may be declared
vacant by the Council, and filled by appointment until the election of a successor. No resignation of any member of the Society
shall become effective unless consented to by the Council.

## ARTICLE XVII.

### Of Disqualifications

No person who may be enrolled as a member of this Society
shall be permitted to continue in membership, when his proofs of
eligibility shall be found to be defective. The Council, after
thirty days notice to such person to substantiate his claim, and
upon his failure satisfactorily so to do, may require the Secretary
to erase his name from the membership list. The said person

shall have the right to appeal to the Society at the next Court, or at the General Court. If the said appeal be sustained by a two-thirds vote of the members present at such Court, the said person's name shall be restored to said membership list.

## ARTICLE XVIII.

### Of Expulsion and Suspension

Any member, for cause, or conduct detrimental or antagonistic to the interests or purposes of the Society, or for just cause, may be suspended or expelled from the Society. But no member shall be suspended or expelled, unless written charges be presented against such member, to the Council. The Council shall give reasonable notice of such charges and afford such member reasonable opportunity to be heard. The Council after hearing such charges, may recommend to the Society the suspension or expulsion of such member, and if the recommendation of the Council be adopted by a majority vote of the members of the Society present at such Court, he shall be suspended or expelled and the insignia of such member shall thereupon be returned to the Treasurer of the Society, and his rights therein shall be suspended or extinguished. The Treasurer shall refund to such member the amount paid for the said insignia.

## ARTICLE XIX.

### Of the Courts

The General Court of the Society shall be held on the twenty-first day of December in each year, being the anniversary of the landing of the Pilgrims. When that date occurs on Sunday the General Court shall be held on the preceding Saturday. Special Courts may be held at the call of the Governor, and shall be held at the written request of five members of the Society. All notices for Courts shall be sent out at least six days before the date of such Courts. Ten members of the Society shall constitute a quorum of the General Court and of Special Courts.

## ARTICLE XX.

### Of Service of Notice

It shall be the duty of every member to inform the Secretary of his place of residence, and of any change thereof, and of his post office address.

Service of any notice, under the Constitution and By-Laws, on any member, addressed to his last post office address, forwarded by mail, shall be sufficient service of notice.

## ARTICLE XXI.

### Of Certificates of Membership

Members may receive a certificate of membership which shall be signed by the Governor, Secretary and Registrar.

## ARTICLE XXII.

### Of the Nominating Committee

The Society shall, at some Court of the Society other than the General Court, elect by written ballot a nominating committee, of five members, none of whom shall be officers or members of the Council.

It shall be the duty of the nominating committee, to select the name of a candidate for each office to be filled at the ensuing

General Court, and to notify the Secretary of the Society of the names selected, at least fifteen days before the General Court.

It shall be the duty of the Secretary, to mail to each member of the Society, at least ten days before the General Court, a copy of the report of the Nominating Committee.


## ARTICLE XXIII.

### Of Alteration or Amendment

No alteration or amendment of the By-Laws shall be made, unless notice shall have been duly given in writing, signed by the member of the Society proposing the same, to the Secretary for presentation to the Court. The Secretary shall send a copy of the proposed amendment to the members of the Council, and state the date of the meeting at which the same will be voted upon.

No amendment or alteration shall be made, unless adopted by a two-thirds vote of the members present at the Council voting upon the same.

# Officers

OF THE

## GENERAL SOCIETY OF COLONIAL WARS

### 1905-1907

---

Governor General

ARTHUR J. C. SOWDEN, Boston, Mass.

Deputy Governors General

California........... SPENCER ROANE THORPE,
                                        Los Angeles

Colorado........... FRANK TRUMBULL,
                                        Denver

Connecticut......... BELA PECK LEARNED,
                                        Norwich

Delaware........... WILLIAM ALEXANDER LA MOTTE,
                                        Wilmington

District of Columbia.. THOMAS HYDE,
                                        Washington

Georgia............ JOHN AVERY GORE CARSON,
                                        Savannah

Illinois............. JOHN SMITH SARGENT,
                                        Chicago

Indiana............ ALEXANDER F. FLEET,
                                        Culver

Iowa............... SAMUEL F. SMITH,
                                        Davenport

Kentucky........... Hon. D. LINN GOOCH,
                                        Covington

Maine..............JOHN M. GLIDDEN,
>                                    New Castle

Maryland...........Gen. JOSEPH L. BRENT,
>                                    Baltimore

Massachusetts........ARTHUR J. C. SOWDEN,
>                                    Boston

Michigan...........THEODORE H. EATON,
>                                    Detroit

Minnesota..........Gen. JAMES FRANKLIN WADE, U. S. A.,
>                                    St. Paul

Missouri............JOHN B. WHITE,
>                                    Kansas City

New Hampshire......Prof. CHARLES LATHROP PARSONS,
>                                    Durham

New Jersey.........EMORY McCLINTOCK,
>                                    Morristown

New York..........WALTER LISPENARD SUYDAM,
>                     43 East Twenty-second St., New York

Ohio...............MICHAEL MYERS SHOEMAKER,
>                                    Cincinnati

Pennsylvania........RICHARD McCALL CADWALADER,
>                                    Philadelphia

Rhode Island........GEORGE CORLIS NIGHTINGALE,
>                                    Providence

Vermont...........ROBERT NOBLE,
>                                    Burlington

Virginia............Hon. RICHARD T. WALKER DUKE, Jr.,
>                                    Charlottesville

Washington.........J. KENNEDY STOUT,
>                                    Spokane

Wisconsin..........WILLIAM WOLCOTT STRONG,
>                                    Racine

# Constitution

## GENERAL SOCIETY OF COLONIAL WARS.

———

### PREAMBLE

WHEREAS, it is desirable that there should be adequate celebrations commemorative of the events of Colonial History, happening from the settlement of Jamestown, Vir., May 13, 1607, to the battle of Lexington, April 19, 1775: Therefore, the Society of Colonial Wars has been instituted to perpetuate the memory of those events, and of the men who in military, naval and civil positions of high trust and responsibility, by their acts of Counsel, assisted in the establishment, defense and preservation of the American Colonies, and were, in truth, the founders of this Nation. With this end in view, it seeks to collect and preserve manuscripts, rolls, relics and records, to provide suitable commemorations or memorials relating to the American Colonial period and to inspire in its members the fraternal and patriotic spirit of their forefathers, and in the community, respect and reverence for those whose public services made our freedom and unity possible.

### ARTICLE I.

#### Name

The Society shall be known by the name and title of The General Society of Colonial Wars.

## ARTICLE II.

### Membership

Any male person above the age of 21 years, of good moral character and reputation, shall be eligible to membership in the Society of Colonial Wars, who is lineally descended, in a male or female line, from an ancestor

(1)   Who served as a military or naval officer or as a soldier, sailor or marine, or as a privateersman under authority of the Colonies which afterward formed the United States, or in the forces of Great Britain, which participated with those of the said Colonies, in any wars in which the said colonies were engaged, or in which they enrolled men from the settlement of Jamestown, May 13, 1607, to the battle of Lexington, April 19, 1775, or

(2)   Who held office in any of the Colonies between the dates above mentioned either as

(a)   Director General, Vice Director General, or member of the Council or legislative body in the Colony of New Netherlands.

(b)   Governor, Lieutenant or Deputy Governor, Lord Proprietor, member of the King's or Governor's Council, or legislative body in the Colonies of New York, New Jersey, Virginia, Pennsylvania and Delaware.

(c)   Lord Proprietor, Governor, Deputy Governor or member of the Council or of the legislative body in Maryland and the Carolinas.

(d)   Governor, Deputy Governor, Governor's Assistant, or Commissioner to the United Colony of New England, or member of the Council, Body of Assistants, or legislative body in any of the New England Colonies.

One collateral representative of an ancestor, such as above specified, shall be eligible to membership, providing there be no existing lineal descendant, and provided that such person be the oldest collateral representative in the male line of such ancestor, or has filed with the Secretary General of the Society, written renunciations from all other persons having nearer claims to representation.

No State Society shall adopt any rule of eligibility for membership which shall admit any person not eligible for membership in the General Society. But any State Society may, except as to members transferred from another State Society, further restrict at its discretion, the basis of eligibility for membership in its own Society.

## ARTICLE III.

### General Society

The General Society of Colonial Wars shall consist of the Societies now existing in the States of New York, Pennsylvania, Maryland, Massachusetts, Connecticut and District of Columbia, and such other State Societies as may from time to time be duly organized and authorized by the General Society.

Whenever the word "State" occurs in this Constitution it shall be held to include within its meaning the territories of the United States and the District of Columbia.

## ARTICLE IV.

### Officers

The Officers of the General Society of Colonial Wars shall be: A Governor General; a Deputy Governor General from each State Society; a Secretary General; a Deputy Secretary

General; a Treasurer General; a Deputy Treasurer General; a Registrar General; a Historian General; a Chaplain General; a Chancellor General and a Surgeon General.

With the exception of the Deputy Governor Generals, the above officers will be elected by a plurality vote of the delegates present at a General Assembly of the Society.

Vacancies occurring by death or resignation may be filled by the General Council for the unexpired term.

Each Deputy Governor General shall be elected by a plurality vote of the delegates present, in the General Assembly, from the State from which said Deputy Governor General is chosen.

The above officers shall serve until the next regular meeting of the General Assembly or until their successors are duly chosen.

## ARTICLE V.

### Meetings

The regular meetings of the General Society shall be termed "General Assembly," and shall be held once every three years, at such time and place as the preceding General Assembly may elect.

Special General Assemblies may be held upon the order of the Governor General, or upon the order of the Governors of three of the State Societies.

General Assemblies shall consist of the General Officers and five delegates from each State Society.

Delegates or General Officers, representing a majority of the State Societies, shall constitute a quorum for the transaction of business, and proceedings shall be in accordance with parliamentary law.

The order of business shall be:

FIRST. The calling of the General Assembly to order by the Governor General, or in his absence, by the Secretary General.

SECOND. Prayer by the Chaplain General.

THIRD. Reading of minutes of last General Assembly.

FOURTH. Report from Secretary General.

FIFTH. Report from Treasurer General.

SIXTH. Reports from Committees and Officers.

SEVENTH. Unfinished Business.

EIGHTH. New Business.

NINTH. Reports from State Societies.

TENTH. Election of Officers.

ELEVENTH. Benediction by the Chaplain General.

The Minutes of each assembly shall be read before its final adjournment.

## ARTICLE VI.

### State Societies

Each State Society shall annually transmit to the Secretary General a circular letter, stating the number of its members, general matters of interest, and any suggestions which may be deemed of advantage to the Society.

Each State Society shall in the month of January in each year, pay to the Treasurer General the sum of $25.00.

## ARTICLE VII.

### Powers of the General Society

The General Society shall have sole power of action in the National as distinct from the State affairs of the organization. It shall have jurisdiction to pass upon all questions of eligibility referred to it by the Registrar General, but shall not otherwise interfere in the regulations or government of any State Society, unless by a plurality vote of the General Assembly, when the surrender of a State Charter may be demanded, should an investigation show that such action is necessary for the welfare of the Societies at large. It shall have power to grant charters to States other than those in which the Society is already organized, provided, that at least nine persons duly qualified to be members, make such application. It shall issue the insignia and the diplomas of membership. It shall publish the Year Book with the co-operation of the several State Societies, and the cost shall be defrayed by the latter in proportion to their membership.

The General Council, which shall be composed of all the General Officers, shall exercise the powers of the General Society (except those of demanding State Charters and of amending the Constitution) between meetings of the General Assembly, to which latter body it shall regularly report all its transactions.

## ARTICLE VIII.

### Governor General

The Governor General, or in his absence, a duly selected temporary presiding officer, shall preside at all General Assemblies and meetings of the General Council of the Society.

## ARTICLE IX.

### Secretary General

The Secretary General shall be keeper of the Great Seal of the Society and of the General Society flag, and of the diploma. He shall conduct the general correspondence of the Society and keep a record thereof. He shall have charge of the printing and publications of the Society. He shall give due notice of the time and place of the holding of all meetings of the General Assembly and of the General Council and shall keep full record of their proceedings.

## ARTICLE X.

### Treasurer General

The Treasurer General shall collect and keep the funds and securities of the Society and deposit and invest them subject to the direction of the General Council. Out of these funds he shall pay such sums as may be ordered by the General Council. He shall keep a full account of his receipts and payments and at each General Assembly or when required by the General Council, shall render an account of the same. He shall be Custodian of the die of the Insignia and may issue the Insignia and Rosettes. For the faithful performance of his duty he may be required to give such security as the General Council may deem proper.

## ARTICLE XI.

### Registrar General

It shall be the duty of each State Society to file with the Registrar General a duplicate of the application of each member. The Registrar General shall receive and file all duplicate applications upon which membership has been granted, with a list of all diplomas signed by him and all documents which the Society may acquire. It shall also be his duty to submit to the General Council any application for membership which in his opinion does not fulfill the requirements of Article II of this Constitution.

## ARTICLE XII.

### Historian General

The Historian General shall keep a detailed record of all historical and commemorative celebrations of the General Society and shall edit and prepare for publication such historical addresses, papers and other documents as the Society may decide to publish.

## ARTICLE XIII.

### Chaplain General

The Chaplain General shall be an ordained minister of a Christian Church, and it shall be his duty to officiate when called upon by the proper officers.

## ARTICLE XIV.

### Chancelor General

The Chancelor General shall be a lawyer duly admitted to the bar, and it shall be his duty to give legal opinion on matters affecting the Society when called upon by the proper officers.

## ARTICLE XV.

### Surgeon General

The Surgeon General shall be a practising physician.

## ARTICLE XVI.

### Great Seal

The Great Seal of the General Society shall be: Within a beaded annulet, a title scroll, "1607, General Society of Colonial Wars, 1775;" and in base the motto: "Fortiter Pro Patria," surrounding diaper charged with nine mullets. Over all a shield, surmounted of the crown, bearing American Colonial Seals quarterly of nine; I. Virginia; Argent, a cross gules between four escutcheons each regally crowned proper, the first and fourth escutcheons, France and England, quarterly; second escutcheon,

Scotland; third, Ireland. II. New York: Argent, a beaver bendways proper on a bordure tenny, a belt of wampum of the first. III. Massachusetts: Azure, on a mount between two pine trees vert, an Indian affronté or, belted with leaves of the second, holding in his dexter hand an arrow paleways, point downwards, and in his sinister hand a bow paleways, of the third; upon a scroll proper, issuing from his mouth, the legend, "Come over and help us." IV. New Hampshire: Quarterly, first and fourth grand quarter of France and England; second, Scotland; third, Ireland; over all an escutcheon of pretence; azure billetée or, a lion rampant of the second, for Nassau. V. Connecticut: Argent, a dexter hand issuing out of clouds in dexter chief, holding a double scroll proper, fesseways, bearing the legend, "Sustinet qui transtulit;" in base fifteen grape vines, six, five, four, leaved and fructed proper. VI. Maryland: Quarterly first and fourth paly of six or and sable, a bend counterchanged, for Calvert; second and third, per fesse and per pale argent and gules, a cross bottony counterchanged for Crossland (seal of Lord Baltimore). VII. Rhode Island: Azure, an anchor in pale or. VIII. New Jersey: Quarterly, first, England impaling Scotland; second, France; third, Ireland; fourth, per pale and per chevron; first, gules two lions passant guardant in pale or, for Brunswick; second, or, semée of hearts, a lion rampant azure, for Lunenburgh; third, gules, a horse courant argent, for Westphalia; over all an inescutcheon gules charged with the crown of Charlemagne. IX. Pennsylvania: Argent on a fesse sable, three plates (Arms of Penn).

## ARTICLE XVII.

### Insignia

The insignia of the Society shall consist of a badge, pendant by a gold crown and ring, from a watered silk ribbon one inch and a half wide of red, bordered with white and edged with red.

The badge shall be surrounded by a laurel wreath in gold and shall consist of:

Obverse; A white enameled star of nine points bordered with red enamel, having between each star point a shield displaying an emblem of one of the nine original colonies; and, within a blue enameled garter bearing the motto, "Fortiter Pro Patria," an Indian's head in gold relievo.

Reverse; The star above described, but with gold edge, each shield between the points displaying a mullet, and in the center, within an annulet of blue bearing the title, "Society of Colonial Wars, 1607-1775," the figure of a Colonial soldier in gold relievo. The reverse of the crown of each insignia shall bear an engraved number, corresponding to that of the registered number of the member to whom such insignia has been issued.

The insignia shall be worn by the members on all occasions, when they assemble as such, for any stated purpose or celebration, and may be worn on any occasion of ceremony. It shall be worn conspicuously, on the left breast; but members who are, or have been Gentlemen of the Council of a State Society, may place a rosette of regulation pattern, upon the silk ribbon from which it is pendant.

Members who are, or have been General Officers, or Officers of a State Society, may wear the insignia with three jewels in a crown, and suspended from a regulation ribbon around the neck.

Members who are, or have been Governors, Deputy Governors, or Lieutenant Governors of State Societies, or Officers of the General Society, may, in addition to the insignia so suspended, wear a ribbon of the Society's colors, three and one-half inches in width, extending from the right shoulder to the left hip. The insignia shall be worn only as above prescribed.

## ARTICLE XVIII.

### Diploma

The Diploma of this Society shall bear the following words:

## GENERAL SOCIETY OF COLONIAL WARS.

TO ALL WHOM IT MAY CONCERN:

Greeting: Know ye, this is to certify that on the . . . . . . . .
day of . . . . . . . . . . . . . . ., in the year of our Lord . . . . . . . .,
and in the year of this Society, the . . . . . . . . . . . . . . . . . . . .
. . . . . . . . . . . . . . . . . . . . . . . . . . . . . . . . . . . . . . . . . .
Gentleman, was duly elected an Hereditary Member of the
Society of Colonial Wars in the State of . . . . . . . . . . . . . . . .
by right of his descent from . . . . . . . . . . . . . . . . . . . . . . . .

.        In witness whereof: We have hereunto signed
our names and affixed the Great Seal of the General
Society.

Officers of the General Society:

. . . . . . . . . . . . . . . . . . . . . ., Governor-General.
. . . . . . . . . . . . . . . . . . . . . ., Secretary-General.
. . . . . . . . . . . . . . . . . . . . . ., Registrar-General.
And countersigned by the Governor, Secretary, and
Registrar of the State Society.

Bordering the top and left side of the diploma is an orna-
mental scroll work containing within the initial letter "G" of
"General Society," a representation of Captain Miles Standish
and a band of Colonial Soldiery; the initial surmounted by the
Imperial Crown of the British Empire and having below it the
motto of the Society.   Ranged along the scroll are shields bearing the arms of the original nine Colonies, as emblazoned in the
Great Seal of the Society, and around these are emblems of
colonial warfare with the flags of Sweden and New Netherland,
and the rose, thistle, shamrock and corn-flower, badges respec-

tively of England, Scotland, Ireland and Germany. At the center at top, is a cluster of Indian weapons and the head of a Sachem charged upon the Fleur-de-lis of France.

## ARTICLE XIX.

### Flag

The flag of this Society shall consist of the red cross of St. George on a white field, bearing in the center the escutcheon of the General Society, surmounted by the crown and surrounded by nine stars.

## ARTICLE XX.

### State Secretaries

It shall be competent for the General Council to appoint State Secretaries in States where no State Societies exist, with a view to represent the interest of this Society, and if authorized to do so, to prepare for the organization of new State Societies. Such State Secretaries shall be subject to the direction and regulation of the General Council. Their appointment shall be for a limited time, not to exceed one year, but may be renewed. They may be removed for cause, and their office shall terminate upon the organization of, and grant of a charter to a Society in their State. They shall communicate with, and receive communication from the Society through the Secretary General.

## ARTICLE XXI.

### Members of State Societies

The General Council shall elect to membership only charter members of new State Societies, whose membership shall be ipso facto transferred to their own State Society with the grant of its charter.

No State Society shall elect to membership, persons resident within the territory of another State Society, except upon written consent given in advance, by the Council of the latter Society. But members changing residence from one State to another, or coming within the jurisdiction of a new State Society, may at their option, retain membership in the State Society in which they were originally admitted. A member of any State Society, may be admitted to membership, by action of the Council of another State Society, within the bounds of which he is resident, upon satisfactory proof of his membership in good standing in the Society from which he comes, and subject to the rules and regulations of the Society he enters.

An initiation fee shall not be twice required.

## ARTICLE XXII.

### Alterations and Amendments

No alterations of, or amendments to this Constitution shall be made, unless proposed by the Council of a State Society in writing. The Secretary General shall send a printed copy of the proposed amendment to each State Society, naming the time when, and the place where it will be voted upon, and the voting shall take place in the General Assembly.

Six months notice shall be given to each Society.

No amendment shall be made, unless adopted by a two-thirds vote of the State Societies, through their delegates in the General Assembly.

# In Memoriam

---

## CHANDLER PEASE CHAPMAN

Born in Bristol, Ohio, Feb. 13th, 1844.
Died in Madison, Wis., May 12th, 1897.

## JAMES KNEELAND

Born in LeRoy, N. Y., Feb. 12, 1816.
Died in Milwaukee, Wis., Sept. 6th, 1899.

## BEDFORD BROWN HOPKINS

Born in Clarence, N. Y., Oct. 16th, 1834.
Died in Milwaukee, Wis., Dec. 3d, 1903.

## HENRY CLAY PAYNE

Born in Ashfield, Mass., Nov. 23d, 1843.
Died in Washington, D. C., Oct. 4th, 1904.

## HAROLD GREEN UNDERWOOD

Born in Litchfield, N. Y., Aug. 1st, 1852.
Died in Chicago, Ill., May 12th, 1905.

# Membership Roll

# Membership Roll

Wisconsin No.                                    Society No.

## 1    WILLIAM WOLCOTT STRONG    896

Born March 3, 1852, Chicago, Ill.

Generation.    Line of Descent from William Bradford.

9   William Sumner Strong (1820-1888) Adaline Sophia Irwin (1823-1874).
8   William Strong (1785-1841) Naomi Terry (1787-1869).
7   Samuel Terry (1750-1838) Huldah Burnham (1752-1809).
6   Samuel Terry (1725-1798) Mary Kellogg (1730-1801).
5   Ephraim Terry (1701-1783) Anne Collins (1702-1778).
4   Nathaniel Collins (1677-1756) Alice Adams (1682-1735).
3   William Adams (1650-1685) Alice Bradford (——1680).
2   William Bradford² (1624-1704) Alice Richards (——1671).
1   William Bradford¹ (1588-1659) Alice Carpenter (1591-1670).


WILLIAM BRADFORD². Commanded the Expedition to relieve Swansey, 1675. Wounded by the Indians in the "Great Swamp Fight." Deputy Governor of Plymouth.

Palfrey's History of New England, Vol. II, pp. 131-148-387-408.
Bodge's Soldiers in King Philip's War, p. 70.


WILLIAM BRADFORD¹. One of the signers of the Mayflower Compact, 1620. Governor of Plymouth Colony in 1621-1632-1637-1639-1642-1648-1656.

Bancroft's History of the United States, Vol. I, pp. 210-211.
Palfrey's History of New England, Vol. I, p. 408.

(Supplemental.)

### LINE OF DESCENT FROM ROGER WOLCOTT.

Generation.

5  William Sumner Strong (1820-1888) Adaline Sophia Irwin (1823-1874).
4  William Strong (1785-1841) Naomi Terry (1787-1869).
3  John Strong (1760-1836) Lydia Sumner (1759-1818).
2  John Strong (1707-1793) Hepsibah Wolcott (1707-1780).
1  Roger Wolcott (1678-1762) Sarah Drake (1686-1747).

ROGER WOLCOTT[1] of Windsor, Conn. Commissary in Queen Anne's War in 1711. Commanded the Connecticut troops in the Louisburg Expedition and was second in command of the United Colonial Army in 1745. Governor of Connecticut, 1750-54.

Stiles' History of Ancient Windsor, p. 217.
Hollister's History of Connecticut, Vol. I, pp. 400-495.

JOHN STRONG[2] of Windsor, Conn. Drummer in Capt. Benjamin Allyn's Company in the Crown Point Expedition, August, 1755. Ensign in General Phineas Seymour's Command, Siege of Montreal, 1760.

Stiles' History of Ancient Windsor, pp. 251-269.
Connecticut War Archives, Vol. VI.

State No.                                          Society No.

2            FRANK SLOSSON.            1659

Born October 18, 1846, Richmond, Mass.

Generation.       Line of Descent from James Avery.

7  Martin Slosson (——) Sabra Avery (1802——).
6  Russell Avery (1769-1831) Betsy Wheeler (——).
5  Thomas Avery (1746——) Hannah Smith (1745-1813).
4  Christopher Avery, Jr. (1709-1778) Eunice Prentice (1716-1796).
3  Christopher Avery (1679-1753) Abagail Park (——1713).
2  James Avery, Jr. (1646-1748) Deborah Stallyon (——1729).
1  James Avery (1620-1700 Joanna Greenslade (1622——).

JAMES AVERY.[1]  Ensign, Lieutenant and Captain. Second in command under Capt. John Winthrop. Captain in

1673, in command of a force of 100 Dragoons. Commanded the Pequot Allies in "The Great Swamp Fight."

> Sweet's Averys of Groton, pp. 14-26.
> Register Society of Colonial Wars, 1896, p. 279.

State No.

Society No.

## 3    †CAPT. PHILIP READE, U. S. A.    522

### Born October 13, 1844, in Lowell, Mass.

Generation.        Line of Descent from John Perkins.

9  Henry Reade (1804-1878) Rowena Hildreth (1814——).
8  Israel Hildreth (1791-1859) Dolly Jones (1792-1858).
7  Israel Hildreth (1755-1839) Susannah Hale (——).
6  Ezekiel Hale (1725-1789) Abigail Sargent (1734-1818).
5  Christopher Sargent (1704-1790) Susannah Peaslee (1712-1785).
4  Thomas Sargent² (1676-1719) Mary Stevens (1679-1766).
3  Thomas Sargent¹ (1643-1705) Rachel Barnes (——).
2  William Sargent (1602-1678) Elizabeth Perkins (——).
1  John Perkins (1590-1654) Judith ——— (——).

SERGEANT JOHN PERKINS¹ of Agawam (Ipswich)', Mass. Bay Colony. Sergeant of the allied English and the friendly aboriginal Indians under their Chief, Masconomo, at Agawam, during the war with the Tarratines, July to September, 1631. In March, 1650, Sergeant John Perkins, senior, of Ipswich, "being above 60 years of age, was freed from ordinary training by the Court."

> Town Records of Ipswich.
> Mather's Early History of New England, p. 111.
> Perkins' The Family of John Perkins of Ipswich, 1889, p. 4.
> Nason's History of Ipswich.
> Governor John Winthrop's Journal.
> The Anchoring of the Fleet at Cape Ann in 1630.
> History of Essex County, Mass., Chapter "Ipswich," p. 200.

†Life Member.

(Supplemental.)

## LINE OF DESCENT FROM FRANCIS COOKE.

Generation.

8  Henry Reade (1804-1878) Rowena Hildreth (1814——).
7  William Reade[6] (1758-1829) Lydia B. Nourse (1759-1813).
6  William Reade[4] (1724-1769) Lucy Spaulding (1744-1821).
5  William Reade[8] (1704——) Hannah Bates (1700——).
4  William Reade[2] (1682-1753) Alice Nash (1685-1751).
3  William Reade[2] (1639-1706) Esther Thompson (——).
2  John Thompson (1616-1696) Mary Cooke (——1715).
1  Francis Cooke (1583-1663) ——————————.

FRANCIS COOKE[1] of Plymouth, Dartmouth and Middleborough, Mass. Came over in the Mayflower. Was one of the signers of the original Mayflower compact at Cape ' Cod, Mass., Nov. 11, 1620. A voluntary member of the military company which chose Miles Standish captain, Feb. 17, 1620. Served in expedition against Indians under the latter, Feb. 16, 1621. Member of Plymouth Military Company, June 22, 1644.

> Savage's Genealogical Dictionary, Vol. I, pp. 445-6.
> Davis' Ancient Landmarks of Plymouth, 1893, pp. 69, 340.
> Thompson's Descendants of John Thompson of Plymouth, Mass., 1890, p. 235.
> Bartlett's Pilgrim Fathers of New England, 1853, p. 131.
> Town Records of Plymouth, 1636 to 1705, Vol. I, p. 17.
> Baylies' History of New Plymouth, 1886, Vol. I, pp. 87-88; also pp. 17-18.
> Bradford's History of Plymouth Plantation, 1856, p. 43.
> Reed's History of the Reed-Reade Family, 1861, p. 311.
> Society of Colonial Wars Year Book, 1896, p. 305.

(Supplemental.)

## LINE OF DESCENT FROM WILLIAM READE.

Generation.

7  Henry Reade (1804-1878) Rowena Hildreth (1814——).
6  William Reade (1758-1829) Lydia B. Nourse (1759-1813)
5  William Reade (1724-1769) Lucy Spaulding (1744-1821).
4  William Reade (1704-1773) Hannah Bates (1700——).
3  William Reade (1682-1753) Alice Nash (1685-1751).
2  William Reade (1639-1706) Esther Thompson (——).
1  William Reade (1605-1663) Iris ——————— (——).

WILLIAM READE[5] of Dunstable and Chelmsford, Mass., and Litchfield, Read's Ferry, N. H. Ensign 1761-1764, during part of Fourth
French and Indian War. Lieutenant from 1764-68. Captain from 1768
until his death. Had just received a Colonel's commission at the time of
his decease. Contemporary of Maj. Samuel Moor, Capt. Thomas Parker,
Lieut. James Nahors and Lieut. John Parker, all east side Merrimack river.

> Town Records of Litchfield, N. H., Book I, p. 41, 1737;
>     Vol. II, 1768, p. 33, 1769. First Town Book, p.
>     214, 1761, p. 227, 1763; Vol. II, p. 31, 1768, p. 15,
>     1765, p. 9, 1764, pp. 18-20-22, 1765-66, p. 30,
>     1768.
> New Hampshire Archives, official compilation, Bouton,
>     D. D., Vol. IX, p. 479.
> Town papers of New Hampshire, Litchfield, 1772.
> New England Hist. and Gen. Society, Boston.
> Reed's History Reed-Reade Family, 1861, p. 174.
> Dr. McQueston's History of Litchfield, Nashua, N. H.,
>     pub'd in Hist. of Hillsborough Co., N. H., Hurd.
> Registry of Deeds, Exeter, N. H., and East Cambridge,
>     Mass.

WILLIAM READE[4] of Weymouth, Dunstable, Chelmsford and
Westford, Mass. Served under Sir William Pepperell, March 24 to June
17, 1745, in the Louisburg Expedition, Island of Cape Breton. Soldier in
military service, time of the Indian invasion, 1744-5, King George's War,
1744-48. One of the grantees of land in "Narragansett No. 4," renamed
Goffstown, N. H. On May 9, 1770, he was appointed, and again, July 3,
also Dec. 31, 1772, one of the Justices, Inferior Court of Common Pleas,
Massachusetts.

> Town Records of Litchfield, Hillsboro County, N. H.
> New England Hist. and Gen. Register, 1871, Vol. XXV,
>     p. 251.
> Hodgman's History of Westford, 1659-1883.
> Dr. McQueston's History of Litchfield, N. H.
> Massachusetts Civil List for Colonial and Provincial
>     Periods, 1680-1774, Whitmore, A.M., 1870, pp. 78-
>     79, 137-138.
> Stearn's History of Ashburnham, Mass., p. 36.

WILLIAM READE[3] of Weymouth and Abington, Mass. Styled
Captain in Town Records, etc., of Abington, from March 2, 1712, to his

death. In December, 1748, an act was passed at Portsmouth, N. H., granting him land for military services in the Goffstown Rangers, time of the Indian invasion, three years previous.

> Town Records of Abington, Mass.
> Hurd's History of Hillsborough County, N. H., pp. 304-5.
> Reed's History of the Reed-Reade Families, 1861, p. 337.

WILLIAM READE[2]—sometime Reed-Read-Reid—of Wessaguscus, renamed Plymouth, Mass. Trooper under Capt. Thomas Prentice; also under Lieut. Edward Oakes, also under Capt. Isaac Johnson; also of the militia of Weymouth under Capt. William Torrey, 1675 and 1676, Mount Hope campaign. His wife was Esther Thompson of Middleborough, Mass., grand-daughter of Francis Cooke, who came over in the Mayflower in 1620.

> Massachusetts Archives, Vol. LXVII, pp. 226, 2261; also Vol. LXVIII, p. 333.
> Muster and Pay-Rolls of Mr. John Hull, Treasurer at War, Massachusetts Bay Colony.
> Bodge's Soldiers in King Philip's War, 1675-7, 1891, pp. 39-43.
> Historical Sketch No. 2 of the Town of Weymouth, Weymouth Historical Society, 1622 to 1884, Nash, 1885, p. 40.
> New England Hist. and Gen. Reg., Vol. XXV, 1871, p. 378.
> Reed's History of the Reed-Reade Family, 1861, p. 311.
> Boston Probate Office, 1706.

WILLIAM READE[1] of Wessaguscus, renamed Plymouth Plantation, Mass. Came from England with the Rev. Joseph Hull in the Assurance de Lo, in 1635. He was of the Train Band Wessaguscus, and is referred to as Ensign, May 1, 1640, in connection with Lieut. Davenport in the Records of Massachusetts Bay Colony, proceedings affecting the towns of Ipswich and Rowley. Early settler. On Sept. 2, 1635, was chosen Deputy from Weymouth to the General Court, Massachusetts Bay Colony and retained that office in 1636-38. His widow was alloted land Dec. 14, 1663.

> Massachusetts Records, Vol. I, pp. 189-235.
> Nash's Weymouth Historical Society, No. 2, p. 26.
> Reed's History of the Reed-Reade Families, 1861, Chapter VIII.
> William Reade of Weymouth and his Descendants, p. 310.
> New England Hist. and Gen. Register, Vol. XXV, pp. 12, 310 and 378.
> Register Society of Colonial Wars, 1896, p. 378.

(Supplemental.)

## LINE OF DESCENT FROM SIMON WILLARD.

Generation.

6   Oliver Jones (1762-1816) Dolly Clement (1762-1843).
5   Daniel Clement (1730———) Eunice Hunt (1729———).
4   Nathaniel Clement (1696———) Elinor Coburn (1699———).
3   Daniel Coburn (1654-1712) Sarah Blood (1658-1741).
2   Robert Blood (———1701) Elizabeth Willard (———1690).
1   Simon Willard (1605-1676) Mary Sharpe (1614———).


SIMON WILLARD[1] of Concord, Lancaster and Groton, Mass. One of the founders of Concord, Mass., 1630. Lieutenant, 1637. Captain, 1646. Major, 1653. Representative from 1636 to 1654. Was chosen Assistant in 1654 and held the office of Assistant to the time of his death, in 1676. His first military commission was that of Lieutenant-Commandant, March, 1637, in the Train Band of the Provincial forces of Massachusetts Bay Colony. Promoted Captain of the Colonial forces, 1646, and further promoted to Sergeant-Major in command of the Middlesex Regiment in 1653. He continued in command of that regiment for more than twenty-three years. In 1653 the Sergeant-Major was the chief military officer in his county and was next in rank to Sergeant-Major General, who had command of all the military forces in the Colony. The prefix of "Sergeant" fell gradually into disuse in the latter days of the Colony. Middlesex County then, 1653, included seventeen incorporated towns. Major Simon Willard served actively with the Provincial forces in the early Indian wars. Was Commander-in-Chief of the United Colonial forces against Ninigret, Sachem of the Niantics, in 1654-5. Commanded the Middlesex Regiment of Massachusetts troops in the war against the Sachem Philip of Pokanoket. Led the heroic relief at the battle of Brookfield, Mass., Aug. 2, 1675. Fought, defeated and dispersed the Indians who had attacked Groton, March 17, 1676. Was Deputy and Representative to the General Court of the Province of Massachusetts Bay Colony from 1636 to 1654. Chosen Assistant and Councilor under Governors Richard Bellingham, John Endicott and John Leverett, annually, from 1654 to his death in 1676. As a magistrate and judge, Major Simon Willard was a humane man. For his military services the Government made Major Simon Willard a grant of 1,000 acres of land.

> Colonial Records, Province of Massachusetts Bay, pp. 122-152-180-181-187-194-210-214.
> Whitmore's Massachusetts Civil List for the Colonial and Provincial periods, 1630-1774, 1870, pp. 23-24-25.
> Register Society Colonial Wars, 1896, p. 417.

Willard's Memoirs of Life and Times of Major Simon
  Willard, 1858.
Hubbard's Indian Wars, published in 1677.
Mather's History of the War with the Indians, 1675-76.
Shattuck's History of Concord, Mass., 1835.
Barry's History of Massachusetts, p. 347.
Allen's History of Chelmsford, Mass., 1820.


(Supplemental.)

## LINE OF DESCENT FROM RICHARD HILDRETH.

Generation.
7   Henry Reade (1804-1878) Rowena Hildreth (1814——).
6   Israel Hildreth² (1791-1859) Dolly Jones (1792-1858).
5   Israel Hildreth¹ (1755-1839) Susannah Hale (——).
4   Elijah Hildreth (1728-1814) Susannah Barker (1735-1764).
3   Ephraim Hildreth (1680-1740) Mercy Richardson (1689-1743).
2   James Hildreth (1631-1695) Margaret Ward (1659-1693).
1   Richard Hildreth (1605-1693) Sarah ———— (——1644).


EPHRAIM HILDRETH³ of Chelmsford and Dracut, Mass.   Sergeant in 1712; also Sergeant, 1725, in Capt. Eleazor Tyng's Company of
Dunstable, a period of twenty-one weeks of active service, succeeding the
disastrous expedition by Capt. John Lovewell against the Pequawket Indians, May, 1725.   Lieutenant, Dec. 28, 1720; Captain, March 4, 1722,
Major, March 7, 1736.   Major Ephraim Hildreth was town clerk of
Dracut most of the time from 1713 to 1740.   He retained the rank and
title of Major until his death, Sept. 26, 1740.   His grave-stone in the
Hildreth burying-ground of Dracut, now Lowell, Mass., bears the inscrip-
tion:  "Here lies buried the body of Major Ephraim Hildreth," etc.

Town Records of Dracut, Middlesex County, Mass.,
  1710 to 1740; particularly records dated 1720, 1722,
  1736; Vol. I, pp. 160-259, 1740.
Massachusetts Archives, Vol. XLI, p. 196.
Hildreth Records, New England Hist. and Gen. Society,
  Boston, Mass.
Rockingham, N. H., Deeds, Vol. LXVIII, 1738.
Capt. Philip Reade's Origin and Genealogy of the Hil-
  dreth Family of Lowell, Mass., 1892, pp. 1-8-9-11-
  24-25-37 et seq.
Parkman's France and England in North America, part
  sixth, Chapter XI, Lovewell's Fight, p. 258.

RICHARD HILDRETH[1] of old Charlestown Village, Cambridge and Chelmsford, Mass. Was of Cambridge, Mass., May 10, 1643. A grantee of Chelmsford in 1653, where he and his descendants lived from 1653, and in which vicinity his linael descendants still live. Prior to March 3, 1663, was Sergeant in the Military Company at Chelmsford and served until 1664. In 1664 Sergeant Richard Hildreth, "being greatly disadvantaged of the use of his right hand, whereby wholly disabled," received, for the ninth time, an additional grant of land. He was noted in Chelmsford church records about 1670, kept by the Rev. John Fiske, as denying the right of the minister or church committee to compel his attendance at the Meeting House on Sundays and refusing to pay the fines sought to be imposed upon him by the Minister, or Deacon, Esdras Reade, or any other minister or deacon. The record shows that "Sergeant Richard Hildreth used reproachful speech and seditious language concerning the Church." He said that he, and others, had quit England to escape the assumption and interference of the clergy in matters not connected with religion. Their grave-stones are still in the old Chelmsford burying-ground.

> Chelmsford Town Records, Book A, p. 22.
> Gen. Court of the Colony of Massachusetts Bay in New England, Vol. IV, part 2, pp. 100, 1669.
> Allen's History of Chelmsford, 1820.
> New England Hist. and Gen. Reg., Vol. XI, 1857, as corrected, 1892, by Capt. Philip Reade, U. S. A., pp. 4-5-39-40.
> Register Society Colonial Wars, 1896, p. 334.

(Supplemental.)

## LINE OF DESCENT FROM TIMOTHY SPAULDING.

Generation.

5 Henry Reade (1804-1878) Rowena Hildreth (1814——).
4 William Reade[3] (1758-1829) Lydia B. Nourse (1759-1813).
3 William Reade[1] (1724-1769) Lucy Spaulding (1744-1821).
2 Oliver Spaulding (1710-1757) Sarah Read (1709——).
1 Timothy Spaulding (1676-1763) Rebecca Winn (1679-1726).

TIMOTHY SPAULDING[1] of Chelmsford and Westford, Mass. Sergeant in Capt. Timothy Underwood's Company of Col. Prescott's Regiment. Appointed Lieutenant Dec. 10, 1697, shortly after the treaty of Ryswick, Sept. 20, terminating hostilities between France, England, Holland and Spain; close of King William's War.

> Chelmsford Town Records, p. 85, 1697.
> Spalding's Spalding Memorial, Descendants of Edward Spaulding, 1872, p. 52.

(Supplemental.)

### LINE OF DESCENT FROM HENRY FARWELL.

Generation.

7   Henry Reade (1804-1878) Rowena Hildreth (1814——).
6   William Reade³ (1758-1829) Lydia B. Nourse (1759-1813)
5   William Reade² (1724-1769) Lucy Spaulding (1744-1821).
4   William Reade¹ (1704——) Hannah Bates (1700——).
3   John Bates (———) Mary Farwell (———).
2   Joseph Farwell (1642-1722) Hannah Learned (1649-1666).
1   Henry Farwell (———) ——— (———).

HENRY FARWELL¹ of Concord and Chelmsford, Mass. Detailed to defend the Henry Farwell garrison house at Musketaquid; name changed Sept. 2, 1635, to Concord, Mass. First town settled in New England above tide water.

> Chelmsford Town Records, Book A, pp. 128-129-134.
> Concord Records.
> Farwell Ancestral Memorial.
> Dr. Holton's Henry Farwell of Concord and Chelmsford, Mass., 1879.

State No.                                                    Society No.

## 4      *CHANDLER PEASE CHAPMAN.      999

Born Feb. 13, 1844, in Bristol, Ohio.
Died May 12, 1897, at Madison, Wis.

Generation.      Line of Descent from William Bradford¹.

9   Chandler B. Chapman (1815-1877) Mary Eugenia Pease (1811-1896).
8   James Pease (1781-1855) Olive Thompson (1780-1854).
7   James Pease (1754-1844) Lucy Meacham (1756-1844).
6   Ebenezer Pease (1719-1748) Mary Terry (1723 ?).
5   Ephraim Terry (1701-1783) Anne Collins (1702-1778).
4   Nathaniel Collins (1677——) Alice Adams (1682-1735).
3   William Adams (1650-1685) Alice Bradford (———).
2   William Bradford (1624-1704 Alice Richards (1627-1671).
1   William Bradford (1588-1657) Alice Carpenter (——1670).

WILLIAM BRADFORD.¹ Governor of Plymouth Colony in 1621-1632-1637-1639-1643-1648-1656.

> Bancroft's History of the United States.
> Palfrey's History of New England.
> Savage's Genealogical Dictionary.
> Davis' Landmarks of Ancient Plymouth.

*Deceased.

State No.                                          Society No.

## 5    WILLIAM HENRY UPHAM.    1050

Born May 3, 1841, in Westminster, Mass.

Generation.      Line of Descent from Phineas Upham.

6  Alvin Upham (1799-1852) Sarah Derby (1800-1878).
5  Jonathan Upham (1759-1840) Sarah Upham (1761-1850).
4  Jonathan Upham (1724-1802) ——— Corbin (——1816).
3  Samuel Upham (1691-1761) Mary Grover (←———).
2  John Upham (1666-1733) Abigail Haywood (——1717).
1  Phineas Upham (1635-1676) Ruth Wood (——1696).

PHINEAS UPHAM[1] of Weymouth, Mass. Lieutenant in King Philip's War under Capt. Wayte. Later in the Plymouth Company under Capt. Gorham. Also in the Fourth Company Massachusetts Regiment under Capt. Isaac Johnson. In The Great Swamp Fight, Capt. Johnson was killed. Lieut. Upham succeeded him in command and was severely wounded.

Massachusetts Archives, Vol. 68, p. 104.
Military Records, Vol. 1, p. 280.

State No.                                            Society No.

## 6    †WYMAN KNEELAND FLINT.    1051

Born March 4, 1868, in Milwaukee, Wis.

Generation.      Line of Descent from Edward Fuller.

10  John Gardiner Flint (1829-1896) Frances Kneeland (1842——).
9  Moses Kneeland (1809-1864) Ellen Clarinda Martin (1811-1856).
8  David Kneeland[3] (1772-1821) Statira Williams (1777-1811).
7  David Kneeland[1] (1752-1834) Mercy Kneeland (1751-1834).
6  Isaac Kneeland (1716——) Content Rowley (1719——).
5  John Rowley (——) Deborah Fuller (———).
4  Moses Rowley[2] (1654-1735) Mary Fletcher (1667-1764).
3  Moses Rowley[1] (——1705) Elizabeth Fuller (———).
2  Matthew Fuller (——1678) Frances —— (———).
1  Edward Fuller (——1621) Ann —— (——1621).

MATTHEW FULLER[2] of Barnstable, Mass. Eighth Captain after Miles Standish in Plymouth Colony troop, 1675.

†Life Member.

Surgeon of the forces. One of the Council of War for the Colony of Plymouth. Lieutenant in 1652. Surgeon General in the war against the Dutch of New York.

> Bodge's Soldiers in King Philip's War.
> Savage's Genealogical Dictionary, Vol. II, pp. 215-217.
> Miscellaneous Records of Plymouth Colony, Vol. III, pp. 17, 153; Vol. V, p. 136.
> Register Society Colonial Wars in the State of Illinois, p. 81 (1897).

(Supplemental.)

## LINE OF DESCENT FROM WILLIAM THOMAS.

Generation.
10  John Gardiner Flint (1829-1896) Frances Kneeland (1842——).
9   Moses Kneeland (1809-1864) Ellen Clarinda Martin (1811-1856).
8   David Kneeland² (1772-1821) Statira Williams (1777-1811).
7   David Kneeland¹ (1752-1834) Mercy Kneeland (1751-1834).
6   Hezekiah Kneeland (1722-1779) Mercy Pepoon (1727——).
5   Joseph Pepoon (——) Mary Thomas (1705——).
4   Nathaniel Thomas⁴ (——) Mary Appleton (1673——).
3   Nathaniel Thomas³ (1643-1718) Deborah Jacobs (——1696).
2   Nathaniel Thomas² (1606-1675) —— (——).
1   William Thomas (1573-1651) —— (——).

NATHANIEL THOMAS³ of Marshfield, Mass. Representative many years. Captain in King Philip's War. Member of the Governor's Council.

> Savage's Genealogical Dictionary, Vol. IV, pp. 281-282.
> Register Society Colonial Wars in the State of Illinois, p. 142 (1897).
> Bodge's Soldiers in King Philip's War, pp. 30-31-49-51-61-62-66-455-457-462-477.

NATHANIEL THOMAS² of Marshfield, Mass. Captain of the Marshfield Company. Fourth Captain in Plymouth Colony after Miles Standish.

> Savage's Genealogical Dictionary, Vol. IV, p. 281.
> Register Society Colonial Wars in the State of Illinois, p. 142 (1897).
> Bodge's Soldiers in King Philip's War, pp. 455-457.
> Miss Thomas' History of Marshfield, p. 55.

WILLIAM THOMAS[1] of Marshfield, Mass.  Assistant to Governor
Bradford 1642-1643-1644-1647 and 1651.

> Savage's Genealogical Dictionary, Vol. IV, p. 282.
> Register Society Colonial Wars in the State of Illinois,
>     p. 142 (1897).
> Miss Thomas' History of Marshfield.

### (Supplemental.)
## LINE OF DESCENT FROM JOHN CLARK.
Generation.
9  John Gardiner Flint (1829-1896) Frances Kneeland (1842——).
8  Moses Kneeland (1809-1864) Ellen Clarinda Martin (1811-1856).
7  Wait Martin (1785-1857) Clarinda Pearson (1793-1873).
6  Joseph Pierson (1767-1843) Sarah Watrous (1772-1810).
5  Samuel Watrous (1730——) Mary Howd (——).
4  Joseph Watrous (1690-1750) Mary Buell (1696-1750).
3  Abraham Watrous (1644——) Rebecca Clark (1653-1704).
2  John Clark (——1677) Rebecca Parker (——1683).
1  John Clark (——1674) ——— (——).

JOHN CLARK[1] of Saybrook, Ct.  Chosen by Governor Winthrop
patentee of Saybrook of the Royal Charter given to Connecticut by Charles
II.  Is named in the Royal Charter in 1662.  Soldier in the great battle at
Mystic against the Pequots in 1637.  Deputy for 25 years.

> Savage's Genealogical Dictionary, Vol. I, p. 396; Vol.
>     IV, p. 431.
> Dwight's History of Connecticut, p. 154.
> Bancroft's History United States, Vol. II, p. 54.
> Hinman's Early Puritan Settlers, p. 609.   .

### (Supplemental.)
## LINE OF DESCENT FROM JOHN APPLETON.
Generation.
8  John Gardiner Flint (1829-1896) Frances Kneeland (1842——).
7  Moses Kneeland (1809-1864) Ellen Clarinda Martin (1811-1856).
6  David Kneeland[2] (1772-1821) Statira Williams (1777-1811).
5  David Kneeland[1] (1752-1834) Mercy Kneeland (1751-1834).
4  Hezekiah Kneeland (1722-1779) Mercy Pepoon (1727——).
3  Joseph Pepoon (——) Mary Thomas (1705——).
2  Nathaniel Thomas (——) Mary Appleton (1673——).
1  John Appleton (1629-1699) Priscilla Glover (——).

JOHN APPLETON[1] of Ipswich, Mass. Lieutenant in 1653. Captain 1658. Major and Representative 1656 to 1679.

> Savage's Genealogical Dictionary, Vol. I, pp.60-61.
> Register Society Colonial Wars, 1896, p. 277.
> Bodge's Soldiers in King Philip's War, pp. 70-79-83-116-132-139-140.

(Supplemental.)

## LINE OF DESCENT FROM JOHN BUEL.

Generation.

2  Joseph Watrous (1690-1750) Mary Buel (1696-1750).
1  John Buel (1672———) Mary Loomis (1673-1768).
   (See line of descent from John Clark, p. 59, for remainder of this line.)

(Supplemental.)

## LINE OF DESCENT FROM LION GARDINER.

Generation.

8  John Gardiner Flint (1829-1896) Frances Kneeland (1842———).
7  John Gardiner Flint (1797-1880) Sarah Gregg (1797-1883).
6  Jonas Flint (1760-1849) Eunice Gardiner (1766———).
5  John Gardiner (1732-1803) Phoebe Gallup (———).
4  Joseph Gardiner (1697-1752) Sarah Grant (1699-1754).
3  John Gardiner (1661-1738) Mary King (1670-1707).
2  David Gardiner (1636-1689) Mary Leringham (———).
1  Lion Gardiner (1599-1663) Mary Willemson (1601-1665).

LION GARDINER[1] of Gardiner's Island. Lieutenant in English Army. Master of fortification in Leagues of the Prince of Orange. Constructor of Saybrook Fort. In the Pequot War. Lord of the Isle of Wight (now Gardiner's Island).

> Gardner's Lion Gardiner and his Descendants, 1890.
> Register Society of Colonial Wars, 1896.
> Savage's Genealogical Dictionary, Vol. II, p. 226.
> Magazine of American History, Vol. XIII, pp. 1 to 30.

(Supplemental.)

## LINE OF DESCENT FROM JOSEPH PIERSON.

Generation.

7  John Gardiner Flint (1829-1896) Frances Kneeland (1842———).
6  Moses Kneeland (1809-1864) Ellen Clarinda Martin (1811-1856).
5  Wait Martin (1785-1857 Clarinda Pearson (1793-1873).

4  Joseph Pierson (1767-1843) Sarah Watrous (1772-1810).
3  Ephraim Pierson[2] (1730——) Hannah Barrett (——).
2  Ephraim Pierson[1] (1687——) —————— (——).
1  Joseph Pierson (——) Amy Barnes (——1692).

JOSEPH PIERSON[1] Lieutenant in Southampton, L. I., in 1650.

> Early Records of Southampton.
> Howell's History of Southampton, L. I., Archivist, New
> York State Library, New York.
> Pierson Genealogical Records, (1878) p. 23.

(Supplemental.)

## LINE OF DESCENT FROM THOMAS WILLIAMS.

Generation.
7  John Gardiner Flint (1829-1896) Frances Kneeland (1842——).
6  Moses Kneeland (1809-1864) Ellen Clarinda Martin (1811-1856).
5  David Kneeland (1772-1821) Statira Williams (1777-1811).
4  Thomas Williams (1728-1806) Ann Gates (Hart) (——1784).
3  Chas. Williams[2] (1691-1769) Mary Robinson (——1695).
2  Charles Williams[1] (——) —————— (——).
1  Thomas Williams (——) Elizabeth Tait (——).

CHARLES WILLIAMS[3] of Hadley, Mass. Sergeant in Haddam,
Connecticut Company, in Indian Wars.

> East Haddam Records.
> Register Society Colonial Wars in the State of Ilinois,
> p. 156 (1897).

THOMAS WILLIAMS[1] of Plymouth, Mass. Shared in the dis-
tribution of Meadow Lands in 1633. Served in the Pequot War 1637.

> Plymouth Records, Vol. I, pp. 103-15-61.
> Bodge's Soldiers in King Philip's War, pp. 444-445-457.

(Supplemental.)

## LINE OF DESCENT FROM EDWARD HINMAN.

Generation.
7  John Gardiner Flint (1829-1896) Frances Kneeland (1842——).
6  Moses Kneeland (1809-1864) Ellen Clarinda Martin (1811-1856).
5  Wait Martin (1785-1857) Clarinda Pearson (1793-1873).

    4   Nathan Martin (1734-1794) Ellen Bradley (———).
    3   Samuel Martin (1695———) Annis Hinman (1697———).
    2   Benjamin Hinman (1662-1721) Elizabeth Lamb (———).
    1   Edward Hinman (———1681) Hannah Stiles (———).

EDWARD HINMAN.[1]  Sergeant at Arms in the Life Guard of
King Charles the First.  Associated with Capt. John Underhill in military
service against the Indians.

> Hinman's Genealogy of the Puritans.
> Savage's Genealogical Dictionary, Vol. II, p. 426.
> Cathren's History of Ancient Woodbury, pp. 556-557.
> Register Society Colonial Wars in the State of Illinois,
>     p. 93 (1897).

(Supplemental.)

## LINE OF DESCENT FROM PHILIP CURTIS.

Generation.
    7   John Gardiner Flint (1829-1896) Frances Kneeland (1842———).
    6   Moses Kneeland (1809-1864) Ellen Clarinda Martin (1811-1856).
    5   Wait Martin (1785-1857) Clarinda Pearson (1793-1873).
    4   Nathan Martin (1734-1794) Ellen Bradley (———).
    3   Samuel Martin (1695———) Annis Hinman (1697———).
    2   William Seaborn Martin (———1715) Abigail Curtis (1667-1735).
    1   Philip Curtis (———1675) Obedience Holland (1640———).

PHILIP CURTIS[1] of Stratford, Ct.  Lieutenant in Capt. Hinchman's
Company.  Slain by the Indians in an expedition which left Boston in
1675 for rescue of captives taken by the savages at the town of Marl-
borough.  The captives were recovered, but Lieut. Curtis was killed while
leading the assault.

> Savage's Genealogical Dictionary, Vol. I, p. 486.
> Cathren's History of Ancient Woodbury, p. 531.
> Register Society Colonial Wars in the State of Illinois,
>     p. 70 (1897).
> Bodge's Soldiers in King Philip's War, pp. 30-54-55.

(Supplemental.)

## LINE OF DESCENT FROM EDWARD KNEELAND.

Generation.
    7   John Gardiner Flint (1829-1896) Frances Kneeland (1842———).
    6   Moses Kneeland (1809-1864) Ellen Clarinda Martin (1811-1856).
    5   David Kneeland (1772-1821) Statira Williams (1777-1811).

4 David Kneeland (1752-1834) Mercy Kneeland (1751-1834).
3 Hezekiah Kneeland (1722-1779) Mercy Pepoon (1727——).
2 Benjamin Kneeland (1679——) Abigail ——————— (——————).
1 Edward Kneeland (1640——) Martha ——————— (——————).

EDWARD KNEELAND[1] of Ipswich, Mass. Was in Capt. Whipple's Company in King Philip's War.

> Bodge's Soldiers in King Philip's War, pp. 155-283.
> Register Society Colonial Wars in the State of Illinois,
> p. 103 (1897).

(Supplemental.)

LINE OF DESCENT FROM EDWARD OAKES.

Generation.

7 John Gardiner Flint (1829-1896) Frances Kneeland (1842——).
6 John Gardiner Flint (1797-1880) Sarah Gregg (1797-1883).
5 Jonas Flint (1760-1849) Eunice Gardiner (1766——).
4 Thomas Flint[2] (1722-1802) Eunice Howe (1727-1796).
3 Thomas Flint[1] (1682-1755) Mary Brown (1692——).
2 John Flint (——1686) Mary Oakes (——1690).
1 Edward Oakes (1604-1689) Jane ——————— (——————).

EDWARD OAKES[1] of Concord, Mass. Representative 17 years. Quartermaster of the troops in 1656. Lieutenant in Captain Thomas Prentice's Company in King Philip's War, 1675-6.

> History of Cambridge, p. 616.
> Savage's Genealogical Dictionary, p. 302.
> Register Society Colonial Wars in the State of Illinois,
> p. 116 (1897).
> Bodge's Soldiers in King Philip's War, pp. 79-80-81-84-
> 85-97-284-436-474.

(Supplemental.)

LINE OF DESCENT FROM THOMAS FLINT.

Generation.

7 John Gardiner Flint (1829-1896) Frances Kneeland (1842——).
6 John Gardiner Flint (1797-1880) Sarah Gregg (1797-1883).
5 Jonas Flint (1760-1849) Eunice Gardiner (1766——).
4 Thomas Flint[2] (1722-1802) Eunice Howe (1727-1796).
3 Thomas Flint[1] (1682-1755) Mary Brown (1692——).
2 John Flint (——1686) Mary Oakes (——1690).
1 Thomas Flint (1603-1653) Abigail (——————).

JOHN FLINT.[2]   Lieutenant in Capt. Thomas Hinchman's troop. Deputy to General Court for Elections held at Boston, May 23, 1677. Deputy to the General Court from Concord, Mass., for a series of years.

> Official Records of the General Court of Massachusetts, Vol. 5, pp. 132-142-210-260-350-351.
>
> Cochrane's History of Antrim, N. H., p. 495.
>
> A Genealogical Register of the Descendants of Thomas Flint, of Salem, compiled by John Flint and J. H. Stone.

THOMAS FLINT[1] of Concord, Mass. Magistrate for many years. One of the first settlers of Concord.

> Savage's Genealogical Dictionary, p. 175.
>
> New England Hist. and Gen. Reg., Vol. I, p. 286.
>
> Register Society Colonial Wars in the State of Illinois, p. 79 (1897).

State No.                                                        Society No.

# 7          WILLIAM WARD WIGHT.          1049

Born January 14, 1849, in Troy, N. Y.

Generation.          Line of Descent from Matthew Allyn.

9  William Ward Wight (1821-1868) Lydia Ann Poitevin Van Akin (1824-1893).

8  Simeon Van Akin (1789-1881) Lydia Poitevin (1792-1826).

7  Thomas Poitevin (1756-1824) Martha Stiles (1760-1822).

6  Rev. Thomas Poitevin (1731-1802) Abigail Mosely (1733-1759).

5  Abner Moseley (1699——) Elizabeth Lyman (1702——).

4  Joseph Moseley (1670-1719) Abigail Root (1680——).

3  John Moseley (——1690) Mary Newberry (1648——).

2  Benjamin Newberry (——1689) Mary Allyn (——1703).

1  Matthew Allyn (1604-1671) Margaret Wyatt (————).

JOHN MOSELEY.[3]   Lieutenant in King Philip's War.

> Savage's Genealogical Dictionary.

BENJAMIN NEWBERRY.[2]   Captain in King Philip's War.  Also Lieutenant of Foot Company at Westfield.

> New England Hist. and Gen. Reg., Vol. 25, p. 72; Vol. 8, p. 329.
>
> Moseley Family Memorial, p. 21.
>
> Wight's "The Wights," pp. 225-226.
>
> Savage's Genealogical Dictionary.
>
> Baldwin's Candee Genealogy, pp. 121-127.

MATTHEW ALLYN.[1]  Moderator of Connecticut and
New Haven on their union in 1666.  Deputy to Massachusetts
General Court, 1636, Connecticut, General Court, 1648-57.
Assistant, 1658-67.

> Baldwin's Candee Genealogy, pp. 121-127.
> Register Society Colonial Wars in the state of Illinois.
> Register Society Colonial Wars.
> Stiles' Ancient Windsor.

State No.                                                     Society No.

# 8          ELLIS BAKER USHER.          1915

Born June 21, 1852, Buxton, Maine.

Generation.          Line of Descent from John Lane.

6  Isaac Lane Usher (1825-1889) Susannah Coffin Woodman (1824-1880).
5  Ellis Baker Usher (1785-1855) Hannah Lane (1795-1889).
4  Isaac Lane (1765-1833) Ruth Merrill (1763-1799).
3  Daniel Lane (1740-1811) Mary Woodman (1742-1817).
2  John Lane (1701-1756) Mary Nowell (———).
1  Capt. John Lane (———) Joanna Davidson (———).

DANIEL LANE.  Enlisted under his father, Capt. John
Lane, 1756.  Took part in the Crown Point Expedition.  Only
soldier from Narragansett, No. 1, at the Siege of Quebec under
General Wolf.  Captain in the Revolution.

> The Woodmans of Buxton, Maine.

JOHN LANE.[2]  Celebrated Indian fighter between 1730
and 1750.  Was mustered out after the Siege of Louisburg.
Died at Crown Point.

> Buxton Centennial.
> Massachusetts Archives, Vol. 94.
> Goodwin's Narragansett, No. 1.
> Chapman's Lane Family.

JOHN LANE.[1]  Soldier in King Philip's War under Captain Poole.

> Coffin's History of Newbury, p. 307.
> William's History of Maine,
> Bodge's Soldiers in King Philip's War, p. 259.
> Newbury Town Records.

(Supplemental.)

## LINE OF DESCENT FROM TRISTRAM COFFIN.

Generation.

4   John Lane (————) Joanna Davison (1677——).
3   Daniel Davison (————) Abigail Coffin (————).
2   Peter Coffin (————) Abigail Starbuck (————).
1   Tristram Coffin (1609-1681) Dionis Stevens (————).

Tristram Coffin of Nantucket and Salisbury, died in Nantucket in 1681.

Lane Family, Vol. I, p. 229.
Coffin's History of Newbury.
Bodge's Soldiers in King Philip's War, pp. 211,217,362.
Goodwin's Narragansett, No. 1.
Woodmans of Buxton, Me., p. 27.
Register Society Colonial Wars, 1898, for Hon. Peter and Tristram Coffin.

(Supplemental.)

## LINE OF DESCENT FROM JOHN TILLEY.

Generation.

9   Isaac Lane Usher (1825-1889) Susannah Coffin Woodman (1824-1880).
8   Joseph Woodman (1783-1857) Susanna Coffin (1783-1833).
7   Rev. Paul Coffin (1738-1821) Mary Gorham (1740-1803).
6   Nathaniel Gorham (1709——) Mary Soule (————).
5   Stephen Gorham (1683-1743) Elizabeth Gardner (————1763).
4   John Gorham (1652-1716) Mary Otis (1654-1732).
3   John Gorham (1621-1676) Desire Howland (1623-1683).
2   John Howland, the Pilgrim, (1592-1673) Elizabeth Tilley (1607-1687).
1   John Tilley, the Pilgrim, (————) Bridget Van de Velde (————).

JOHN TILLEY, the Pilgrim, was a citizen of Plymouth and died in 1621.

Wisconsin Year Book.
Register Society of Colonial Wars, for Tilley, Howland and Gorham lines, 1898.

State No.                                                              Society No.

# 9    WILLIAM CHESTER SWAIN.    1916

Born April 22, 1832, in Halifax, Vt.

Generation.        Line of Descent from Peter Bulkeley.

7  Chipman Swain (1795-1873) Dency Gilbert (1796-1867).
6  Joseph Swain (1754-1831) Meliscent Barrett (1759-1838).
5  James Barrett² (1733-1799) Meliscent Estabrook (1738——).
4  James Barrett¹ (1710-1779) Rebecca Hubbard (1717-1806).
3  Joseph Hubbard (1688-1768) Rebecca Bulkeley (1696-1772).
2  Joseph Bulkeley (1670——) Rebecca Jones (1662-1712).
1  Peter Bulkeley (1643-1688) Rebecca Wheeler (1649——).


## COL. JAMES BARRETT.⁴  Colonel of Middlesex
Militia.  Deputy many years.

Register Society Colonial Wars, 1896, p. 281.
Potter's Old Families of Concord.


## MAJOR PETER BULKELEY¹ of Concord, Mass.
Deputy four terms.  Speaker of the House, 1676.  Governor's
Assistant, 1677 to 1685.

Register Society Colonial Wars, 1896.
Potter's Old Families of Concord.


(Supplemental.)

### LINE OF DESCENT FROM JOHN HOWLAND.

Generation.

7  Chipman Swain (1795-1873) Dency Gilbert (1796-1867).
6  Joseph Swain² (1754-1831) Meliscent Barrett (1759-1838)
5  ‡Joseph Swain¹ (1723-1792) Elizabeth Chipman (1719-1773).
4  John Chipman² (1690-1775) Rebecca Hale (1701-1751).
3  Samuel Chipman (1661-1723) Rebecca Cobb (1664-1742).
2  John Chipman¹ (1614-1708) Hope Howland (1629-1683).
1  John Howland (1592-1673) Elizabeth Tilley (1607-1687).

‡This Swain is given special notice in the line of descent from
Jeremiah Swain.

JOHN HOWLAND[1] of Plymouth Colony, 1620. One of the thirteen signers of the Mayflower compact. Was in the "First Encounter" Dec. 8, 1620. Was one of Miles Standish Company. Assistant, 1633 and 1635. Deputy to General Court, 1641.

> Register Society Colonial Wars, 1896, p. 338.
> Bodge's Soldiers in King Philip's War, p. 1.

(Supplemental.)

## LINE OF DESCENT FROM JOHN HALE.

Generation.

6  Chipman Swain (1795-1873) Dency Gilbert (1796-1867).
5  Joseph Swain[2] (1754-1831) Meliscent Barrett (1759-1838).
4  Joseph Swain[1] (1723-1792) Elizabeth Chipman (1719-1773).
3  John Chipman (1690-1775) Rebecca Hale (1701-1751).
2  Robert Hale (1668-1719) Elizabeth Clark (1684-1762).
1  John Hale (1636-1700) Rebecca Byles (——1683).

Rev. JOHN HALE[1] of Charlestown, Mass. Chaplain of the Expedition against Canada in 1690.

> Register Society Colonial Wars, 1896, p. 329.
> Stone's History of Beverly, Mass., p. 43.

(Supplemental.)

## LINE OF DESCENT FROM HUMPHREY BARRETT.

Generation.

6  Chipman Swain (1795-1873) Dency Gilbert (1796-1867).
5  Joseph Swain (1754-1831) Meliscent Barrett (1759-1838).
4  James Barrett[2] (1733-1799) Meliscent Estabrook (1738——).
3  James Barrett[1] (1710-1779) Rebecca Hubbard (1717-1806).
2  Benjamin Barrett (1681-1728) Lydia Minott (1687——).
1  Humphrey Barrett (1630-1716) Mary ——— (1656-1713).

HUMPHREY BARRETT[1] of Concord, Mass. Deputy to General Court, 1691. Ensign, 1688.

> Register Society Colonial Wars, 1896, p. 281.

(Supplemental.)

## LINE OF DESCENT FROM JAMES MINOTT.

Generation.

6  Chipman Swain (1795-1873) Dency Gilbert (1796-1867).
5  James Swain (1754-1831) Meliscent Barrett (1759-1838).
4  James Barrett² (1733-1799) Meliscent Estabrook (1738——).
3  James Barrett¹ (1710-1779) Rebecca Hubbard (1717-1806).
2  Benjamin Barrett (1681-1728) Lydia Minott (1687——).
1  James Minott (1653-1735) Rebecca Wheeler (1666-1734).

JAMES MINOTT.¹ Captain of Concord Militia, 1684. Deputy to General Court, 1700.

> Register Society Colonial Wars, 1896, p. 360.
> Potter's Old Families of Concord.

(Supplemental.)

## LINE OF DESCENT FROM JEREMIAH SWAIN.

Generation.

6  Chipman Swain (1795-1873) Dency Gilbert (1796-1867).
5  Joseph Swain² (1754-1831) Meliscent Barrett (1759-1838).
4  Joseph Swain¹ (1723-1792) Elizabeth Chipman (1719-1773).
3  John Swain (1698-1771) Mary Perkins (——1737).
2  Benjamin Swain (1669-1747) Margaret ——— (——1713).
1  Jeremiah Swain (1643-1710) Mary Smith (1648——).

JOSEPH SWAIN.⁴ Chaplain of Col. Plaisted's Regiment in the Expedition to Crown Point.

> Certified Massachusetts Records, Vol. 94, p. 479.

JOHN SWAIN.³ Sergeant in Capt. Fay's Company, raised for the reduction of Canada, 1758.

> Certified Massachusetts Records, Vol. 96, p. 419.

JEREMIAH SWAIN¹ of Charlestown, Mass. Lieutenant in 1675. Wounded at the Narragansett fight. Captain in 1676. Had large grants of lands for his services in the Indian War. In 1689, Commander-in-Chief of Expedition against the Eastern Indians in Maine. Was Representative, Deputy and Governor's Assistant.

> Official Records of Massachusetts.
> Bodge's Soldiers in King Philip's War.
> Swain's Swain and Allied Families, pp. 6-13.
> Eaton's History of Reading, Mass.

State No.                                                        Society No.

10            *JAMES KNEELAND.                       1917

Born February 12, 1816, in Le Roy, N. Y.
Generation.    Line of Descent from Edward Kneeland (Neland).
5   David Kneeland² (1772-1821) Catherine Pierson (1791-1882).
4   David Kneeland¹ (1752-1834) Mercy Kneeland (1751-1834).
3   Isaac Kneeland (1716——) Content Rowley (1719——).
2   Benjamin Kneeland (1679-1744) Abigail ——— (———).
1   Edward Kneeland (1640-1711) Martha Fowler (———).


EDWARD KNEELAND¹ of Ipswich, Mass.  Soldier in
Capt. Whipple's Company in King Philip's War.

Bodge's Soldiers in King Philip's War, 1896, p. 283.
Pay Rolls of June and August, 1676.


(Supplemental.)

LINE OF DESCENT FROM EDWARD FULLER.

Generation.
8   David Kneeland² (1772-1821) Catherine Pierson (1791-1882).
7   David Kneeland¹ (1752-1834) Mercy Kneeland (1751-1834).
6   Isaac Kneeland (1716——) Content Rowley (1719——).
5   John Rowley (———) Deborah Fuller (———).
4   Moses Rowley² (1654-1735) Mary Fletcher (1667-1764).
3   Moses Rowley¹ (——1705) Elizabeth Fuller (———).
2   Matthew Fuller (——1678) Frances ——— (———).
1   Edward Fuller (——1621) Ann ——— (——1621).


MATTHEW FULLER² of Barnstable, Mass.  Eighth Captain after
Miles Standish in 1675.  Surgeon of the forces, 1673.  One of the Council
of War for the Colony of Plymouth, 1658.  Lieutenant of Military Company of Barnstable in 1652.  Surgeon General of the Expedition against
the Dutch of New York in 1673.

Bodge's Soldiers in King Philip's War.
Savage's Genealogical Dictionary, Vol. II, pp. 215-217.
Records of Plymouth Colony, Vol. III, p. 153; Vol. V,
p. 136.

*Deceased.

(Supplemental.)

## LINE OF DESCENT FROM WILLIAM THOMAS.

Generation.

8  David Kneeland (1772-1821) Catherine Pierson (1791-1882).
7  David Kneeland (1752-1834) Mercy Kneeland (1751-1834).
6  Hezekiah Kneeland (1722-1779) Mercy Pepoon (1727——).
5  Joseph Pepoon (——) Mary Thomas (1705——).
4  Nathaniel Thomas³ (——1738) Mary Appleton (1673-1727).
3  Nathaniel Thomas² (1643-1718) Deborah Jacobs (1643-1696).
2  Nathaniel Thomas¹ (1606-1674) ———— ———— (——).
1  William Thomas (1574-1651) ———— ———— (——).


NATHANIEL THOMAS³ of Marshfield.  Representative many years.  Member of the Governor's Council.  Captain in King Philip's War.

> Savage's Genealogical Dictionary, Vol. IV, p. 281.
> Register Society Colonial Wars, Ill., p. 142.
> Bodge's Soldiers in King Philip's War, pp. 455-457.
> Thomas' History of Marshfield, p. 55.


NATHANIEL THOMAS² of Marshfield, Mass.  Lieutenant in command at New Haven against the Indians.  In 1643 was appointed the fourth Captain in Plymouth Colony after Miles Standish.

> Savage's Genealogical Dictionary, Vol. IV, pp. 281-282.
> Bodge's Soldiers in King Philip's War, pp. 30-31-49-51-61-62-66-455, etc.
> Thomas's History of Marshfield, p. 55.


WILLIAM THOMAS.¹  One of the founders of Plymouth Colony. Assistant to Gov. Bradford, 1642 to 1651.

> Savage's Genealogical Dictionary, Vol. IV, p. 282.
> Register Society Colonial Wars, Ill., p. 142.
> Thomas's History of Marshfield, p. 53.


(Supplemental.)

## LINE OF DESCENT FROM JOHN CLARK.

Generation.

7  David Kneeland (1772-1821) Catherine Pierson (1791-1882).
6  Joseph Pierson (1767-1843) Sarah Watrous (1772-1810).
5  Samuel Watrous (1730——) Mary Howd (——).

4 Joseph Watrous (1690——) Mary Buell (1696-1750).
3 Abraham Watrous (1644——) Rebecca Clark (1653-1704).
2 John Clark (——1677) Rebecca Parker (——1682).
1 John Clark (——1674) ——— ——— (———).

JOHN CLARK[1] of Hartford and Saybrook, Ct. Chosen by Gov. Winthrop as Patentee of Saybrook of the Royal Charter given to Connecticut by Charles II., and is named in the Royal Charter in 1662. Was soldier in the great battle at Mystic against the Pequots in 1637. Deputy for 25 years.

Savage's Genealogical Dictionary, p. 396.
Dwight's History of Connecticut, p. 154.
Hinman's Early Puritan Settlers, p. 609.
Bodge's Soldiers in King Philip's War, p. 466.

(Supplemental.)

LINE OF DESCENT FROM JOHN APPLETON.

Generation.
6 David Kneeland (1772-1821) Catherine Pierson (1791-1882).
5 David Kneeland (1752-1834) Mercy Kneeland (1751-1834).
4 Hezekiah Kneeland (1722-1779) Mercy Pepoon (1727——).
3 Joseph Pepoon (———) Mary Thomas (1705——).
2 Nathaniel Thomas (——1738) Mary Appleton (1673-1727).
1 John Appleton (1622-1699) Priscilla Glover (———).

JOHN APPLETON[1] of Boston, Mass. Lieutenant in 1653. Captain in 1658. Major and Representative, 1656 to 1679. "His resistance to taxation without representation was probably the first instance in the annals of New England."

Savage's Genealogical Dictionary, Vol. I, pp. 60-61.
Bodge's Soldiers in King Philip's War, pp. 70-79-83-116-132, etc.
Register Society Colonial Wars, 1896, p. 277.

(Supplemental.)

LINE OF DESCENT FROM JOSEPH PIERSON.

Generation.
5 David Kneeland (1772-1821) Catherine Pierson (1791-1882).
4 Joseph Pierson (1767-1843) Sarah Watrous (1772-1810).
3 Ephraim Pierson[2] (1730——) Hannah Barrett (———).
2 Ephraim Pierson[1] (1687——) ——— ——— (———).
1 Joseph Pierson (———) Amy Barnes (——1692).

JOSEPH PIERSON.[1]   Lieutenant in Southampton, L. I., in 1650.

> Early Records of Southampton.
> Howell's History of Southampton.
> Pierson's Gen. Records, p. 23.

(Supplemental.)

## LINE OF DESCENT FROM JOHN BUELL.

Generation.
2  Joseph Watrous (1690——) Mary Buell (1696-1750).
1  John Buell (1671——) Mary Loomis (1672-1768).

(See line of descent from John Clark for remainder of this line.)

State No.                                    Society No.

## 11          WILLIAM KING COFFIN.          1852

Born Aug. 9, 1850, in Jacksonville, Ill.

Generation.      Line of Descent from Tristram Coffin.

7  William Coffin (1822-1890) Mary E. Lockwood (1828-1877).
6  Nathaniel Coffin (1781-1864) Mary Porter (1782-1866).
5  James Coffin (1745-1830) Martha McLellan (1745-1825).
4  Edmund Coffin (1708-1789) Shuah Bartlett (——1803).
3  Nathaniel Coffin (1669-1749) Sarah Brocklebank (——1750).
2  Tristram Coffin, Jr., (1632-1704) Judith Greenleaf (1625-1705).
1  Tristram Coffin (1605-1681) Dionis Stevens (——).

TRISTRAM COFFIN.[1]   First Chief Magistrate of the Island of Nantucket.   Was appointed by Gov. Lovelace in 1671.   Again appointed Chief Magistrate in 1677 and served several years.   Court Commissioner, 1655.

> Nantucket Records, Vol. I, p. 201.
> Coffin Family, p. 64.
> New England Hist. and Gen. Reg., Vols. 2 and 24.
> Savage's Genealogical Dictionary.
> Register Society Colonial Wars, 1896, p. 302.

State No.                                              Society No.

## 12          JOHN WILLIAM PETERSON          1918
### LOMBARD.

Born August 3, 1849, in Truro, Mass.

Generation.        Line of Descent from Robert Treat.

7  Lewis Lombard (1801-1879) Sarah Gross (1805-1856).
6  James Lombard (1769-1817) Hannah Snow (1773——).
5  Lewis Lombard (1739-1814) Elizabeth Pike (1739-1818).
4  James Lombard (1703-1769) Elizabeth Freeman (1707-1771).
3  Constant Freeman (1669-1745) Jane Treat (1675-1729).
2  Rev. Samuel Treat (1648-1717) Elizabeth Mayo (1652-1696).
1  Gov. Robert Treat (1624-1710) Jane Tapp (——1703).

ROBERT TREAT.[1]  Commander at "The Great Swamp Fight."  Major commanding Connecticut Troops at Battles of Hadley and Springfield.  Deputy Governor, 1676 to 1686.  Governor, 1686.

Soldiers in King Philip's War, 1896.
Register Society Colonial Wars, 1895, p. 286.


State No.                                              Society No.

## 13               GRANT FITCH.               1919

Born Sept. 22, 1859, in Milwaukee, Wis.

Generation.        Line of Descent from Thomas Fitch.

7  William Grant Fitch (1834-1891) Martha E. Curtiss (1836——).
6  Daniel Grant Fitch (1812-1880) Sarah Miller (1811-1889).
5  Grant Fitch (1782-1848) Millicent Halsey (1789-1829).
4  Haynes Fitch (1735-1815) Anna Cook (1740-1814).
3  James Fitch (1702-1790) Mary Haynes (1699-1789).
2  Thomas Fitch (1671-1731) Rachel ——— (———).
1  Capt. Thomas Fitch (1630-1690) Ruth Clark (———).

THOMAS FITCH[1] of Norwalk, Ct.  Ensign in 1665. King's Commissioner in 1669.  Captain in King Philip's War, 1673.

Register Society Colonial Wars, 1896, p. 317.
Records of the Town of Norwalk, Conn.

State No.                                       Society No.

## 14     CHARLES CURTIS BROWN.    1920

Born May 20, 1854, in Kenosha, Wis.

Generation.     Line of Descent from William Phelps.

8   Charles Curtis Brown (1829-1881) Katharine Jane Lampson (1832-1882).
7   Horace Lampson (1792-1842) Huldah Phelps (1795-1871).
6   Benajah Phelps (1770——) Betsey Graham (———).
5   Abel Phelps (1738——) Lucy Beardsley (———).
4   Capt. Abel Phelps (1705——) Mary ——— (———).
3   Joseph Phelps (1666-1716) Sarah Hosford (1666——).
2   Lieut. Timothy Phelps (1639——) Mary Griswold (1644——).
1   William Phelps (1599-1672) Mary Dover (——1675).

WILLIAM PHELPS.[1] Assistant to the Governor of the Colony of Connecticut from 1639 to 1643.

Hollister's History of Connecticut, Appendix, p. 496.
Register Society Colonial Wars, 1896, p. 371.

State No.                                       Society No.

## 15    NELSON ALONZO PENNOYER.   1921

Born April 3, 1849, in Groton, N. Y.

Generation.     Line of Descent from Preserved Abell.

7   Edgar Pennoyer (1822-1894) Huldah Weed (1821——).
6   Cephas Weed (1785-1858) Anna Baker (1787-1826).
5   Lewis Baker (1761-1814) Lois Walker (1766-1853).
4   Abel Walker (1736-1819) Lois Read (1741-1801).
3   Caleb Walker (1706-1768) Abigail Dean (1704-1795).
2   Ebenezer Walker (1676-1718) Dorothy Abell (1677-1741).
1   Lieut. Preserved Abell (——1724) ——— ——— (———).

PRESERVED ABELL.[1] Served in the Narragansett campaign under Major William Bradford. Lieutenant in Capt. Gallup's Company in Sir William Phips' Expedition against Canada in 1690.

Register Society Colonial Wars, 1896, p. 275.
Bodge's Soldiers in King Philip's War, p. 463.

State No.                                                     Society No.

17        WILLIAM LYMAN MASON.        2095

Born January 21, 1847, in Cincinnati, Ohio.

Generation.        Line of Descent from Thomas Mason.

6  Timothy Battelle Mason (1801-1861) Abigail Hall (1800-1875).
5  Johnson Mason (1767-1856) Caty Hartshorn (1768-1852).
4  Barachias Mason (1723-1795) Love Whitney (1727——).
3  Thomas Mason (1699-1789) Mary Arnold (1703-1798).
2  Ebenezer Mason (1669-1754) Hannah Clark (1666-1757).
1  Thomas Mason (1625-1676) Margery Partridge (——1711).

THOMAS MASON.[1]  Killed in the defense of Medfield
under Lieut. Henry Adams, when that town was partially de-
stroyed by the Indians under "Monaco" in King Philip's War.
Two of his sons were killed at the same time, and a third in the
Indian Wars "to the Eastward" under Capt. Swett.

Tilden's History of Medfield, pp. 429 to 433.
Town Records of Medfield.

(Supplemental.)

LINE OF DESCENT FROM HENRY ADAMS.

Generation.

7  Timothy Battelle Mason (1801-1861) Abigail Hall (1800-1875).
6  Johnson Mason (1767-1856) Caty Hartshorn (1768-1852).
5  Moses Hartshorn (——1776) Elizabeth Smith (1730-1782).
4  Samuel Smith[2] (1700-1763) Silence ——— (——1778).
3  Samuel Smith[1] (1674-1742) Elizabeth Adams (1672-1753).
2  Eleazar Adams (1644-1710) Elizabeth Harding (——1708).
1  Henry Adams (1604-1676) Elizabeth Paine (——1676).

HENRY ADAMS.[1]  A member of the "Ancient and Honorable
Artillery Company" in 1652.  Deputy to the General Court in 1659.
Lieutenant in command at Medfield, Mass., 1676.  Killed by the Indians
under "Monaco" in the attack on Medfield in King Philip's War.

Tilden's History of Medfield.
Bodge's Soldiers in King Philip's War.
Register Society Colonial Wars, 1896.

(Supplemental.)

## LINE OF DESCENT FROM THOMAS STANTON.

Generation.

6  Timothy Battelle Mason (1801-1861) Abigail Hall (1800-1875).
5  Samuel Hall (1757-1828) Sarah Cheney (1758——).
4  Timothy Cheney (1713-1772) Sarah Prentice (1719——).
3  Thomas Prentice[8] (1676-1729) Elizabeth Jackson (1687——).
2  Thomas Prentice[2] (1649-1685) Sarah Stanton (1650-1713).
1  Thomas Stanton (1615-1677) Ann Lord (1621-1688).


THOMAS STANTON.[1]  Special Indian Interpreter to the Colony of
Connecticut.  Interpreter to Gov. John Winthrop before the Pequot War.
Interpreter General to the New England Colonies.  Served in the Pequot
War and rendered valuable service at Saybrook Fort.  Appointed to be
Marshal in 1638.  Deputy to the General Court in 1666.

American Ancestry, Vol. IV, p. 23.
Register Society Colonial Wars, D. C., pp. 26-27-29-30.
Bodge's Soldiers in King Philip's War.


(Supplemental.)

## LINE OF DESCENT FROM THOMAS PRENTICE.

Generation.

1  Thomas Prentice[1] (1621-1710) Grace ——— (———).
   Remainder of this line same as preceding.


THOMAS PRENTICE.[1]  Captain of First Company of Cavalry in
the "Army of the United Colonies."  Gave valuable and efficient service
during King Philip's War and was buried with military honors.  Served in
the Pequot War, in the Narragansett War and in King Philip's War.
Deputy to the General Court in 1672-73.

Pierce's History of Grafton, pp. 547-552.
Jackson's History of Newton, pp. 389-395.
Savage's Genealogical Dictionary, Vol. III, pp. 478-480.
Bodge's Soldiers in King Philip's War, Chapter III.

State No.                                                    Society No.

18        HERBERT WIGHT UNDER-           2096
                    WOOD.

Born February 28, 1855, in Oxford, Mass.

Generation..  '   Line of Descent from John Guild.

8  Albert Gallatin Underwood (1833-1882) Sarah Smith Wight
      (1833——).
7  Alvan Greenleaf Underwood (1808-1885) Emily Amanda Guild
      (1812-1888).
6  Ebenezer Guild (1786——) Hepzibah Russell (——).
5  Ebenezer Guild (1747-1822) Lydia Whittemore (——).
4  Ebenezer Guild (1724-1790) Margaret Pond (——).
3  John Guild (1690——) Mary Foster (——).
2  John Guild (1649-1723) Sarah Fisher (1658——).
1  John Guild (——1682) Elizabeth Crooke (——1669).

JOHN GUILD.[1]   Served in Captain Appleton's Company
in King Philip's War.

Burleigh's Guild Family.
Wight's The Wights.
Register Society Colonial Wars, 1896.
Dedham Historical Registry, Vols. IV and V.


State No.                                                    Society No.

19    ˙   JOHN WYMAN FLINT.           2097

Born October, 1864, in Bellows Falls, Vt.

Generation.      Line of Descent from John Flint.

6  Wyman Flint (1824——) Almira Stickney (1827-1896).
5  John Gardiner Flint (1797-1880) Sarah Gregg (1797-1883).
4  Jonas Flint (1760-1849) Eunice Gardiner (1766——).
3  Thomas Flint, Jr., (1722-1802) Eunice How (1717-1796).
2  Thomas Flint (1682-1755) Mary Brown (1692——).
1  John Flint (——1686) Mary Oakes (——1690).

JOHN FLINT[1] of Concord.   Lieutenant in Capt. Thomas
Hinchman's Troop.   Deputy from Concord.

Official Records of the General Court of Massachusetts,
Vol. 5, pp. 132-210-260-350-351.

Register Society Colonial Wars in the State of Illinois,
    1897, p. 79.
Genealogical Register Descendants of Thomas Flint.
History of Antrim, p. 495.

State No.                                        Society No.

## 20          SAMUEL SWEET SIMMONS.          2098

Born February 11, 1870, in Kenosha, Wis.

Generation.          Line of Descent from William Phelps.

7  Rouse Simmons (1832———) Helen Sophia Lampson (1835———).
6  Horace Lampson (1792-1842) Huldah Phelps (1795-1871).
5  Benajah Phelps (1770———) Betsey Graham (———).
4  Abel Phelps (1738———) Lucy Beardsley (———).
3  Capt. Abel Phelps (1705———) Mary ——— (———).
2  Lieut. Timothy Phelps (1639———) Mary Griswold (1644———).
1  William Phelps (1599-1672) Mary Dover (———1673).


WILLIAM  PHELPS[1] of Windsor, Ct.  Assistant to
Gov. John Webster from 1639-1643.

Hollister's History of Connecticut, Appendix p. 496.
Register Society Colonial Wars, 1896, p. 371.


State No.                                        Society No.

## 21          WILLIAM JAMES STARR.          2172

Born April 20, 1861, in Ripon, Wis.

Generation.          Line of Descent from Thomas Starr.

7  William Starr (1821-1879) Annie Strong (1824———).
6  Samuel Tallman Starr (1780-1820) Lydia Coe Atkins (1779-
    1862).
5  William Starr (1747-1825) Hannah Tallman (1746-1814).
4  Capt. Daniel Starr (1712-1767) Elizabeth Hempsted (1714-1776).
3  Benjamin Starr (1679-1753) Lydia Latham (1686-1747).
2  Comfort Starr (1644-1693) Marah Weld (1646———).
1  Thomas Starr (———1658) Rachel ——— (———).

THOMAS STARR' of Charlestown, Mass.  Surgeon to
the forces sent against the Pequots, May 17, 1637.  Appointed
by the General Court at Boston.  His widow received a grant
of 400 acres of land for his services.

> Colonial Records of Massachusetts.
> Register Society Colonial Wars, 1896, pp. 72-180-393.

State No.                                                    Society No.

## 22          FRANCIS GARDINER FLINT.          2173

Born April 10, 1860, in Bellows Falls, Vt.

Generation.          Line of Descent from John Flint.

6  Wyman Flint (1824——) Almira Stickney (1827-1896).
5  John Gardiner Flint (1797-1880) Sarah Gregg (1797-1883).
4  Jonas Flint (1760-1849) Eunice Gardiner (1766——).
3  Thomas Flint, Jr., (1722-1802) Eunice How (1717-1796).
2  Thomas Flint (1682-1755) Mary Brown (1692——).
1  John Flint (——1686) Mary Oakes (——1690).

JOHN FLINT' of Concord.  Lieutenant in Capt. Thomas
Hinchman's Troop.  Deputy from Concord, Mass.

> Register Society Colonial Wars in the State of Illinois,
>     1897, p. 79.
> Genealogical Register Descendants of Thomas Flint.
> History of Antrim, p. 495.
> Official Records of the General Court of Massachusetts,
>     Vol. 5, pp. 132-210-260-350-351.

State No.                                                    Society No.

## 23          CHARLES GAGER STARK.          2174

Born May 22, 1835, Brattleboro, Vt.

Generation.          Line of Descent from Aaron Stark.

6  Jedediah Lathrop Stark (1793-1862) Hannah Gager (1799-1882).
5  Joshua Stark (1761-1839) Olive Lathrop (1764-1825).
4  Abiel Stark (1724-1770) Chloe Hinckley (——1828).
3  Abiel Stark (———) Mary Walworth (———).
2  Aaron Stark (1654——) Mehitable Shaw (———).
1  Aaron Stark (1602-1685) ——— ——— (———).

AARON STARK[1] of New London, Ct.  Soldier in the Pequot War and in King Philip's War.  Took part in the battle with the Pequots at their fort on the Mystic.  Served under Major John Mason.

> Bodge's Soldiers in King Philip's War.
> Walworth's The Hyde Genealogy, Vol. I, pp. 248-253.

(Supplemental.)

### LINE OF DESCENT FROM SAMUEL LATHROP.

Generation.
6  Jedediah Lathrop Stark (1793-1862) Hannah Gager (1799-1882).
5  Joshua Stark (1761-1839) Olive Lathrop (1764-1825).
4  Jedediah Lathrop (1718-1792) Jemima Birchard (1729-1789).
3  Israel Lathrop[2] (1687-1758) Mary Fellows (———).
2  Israel Lathrop[1] (1659-1733) Rebecca Bliss (———1737).
1  Samuel Lathrop (———1700) Elizabeth Scudder (———).

SAMUEL LATHROP[1] of Scituate.  Soldier in the Narragansett Wars.  "Uncas, hunted by the Narragansetts, had been chased into the fort at the head of the Nahontick and was there besieged; Lieut. James Avery, Mr. Bruster, Samuel Lathrop and others, well armed, succeeded in throwing themselves into the fort, and aided in the defense."

> Lathrop Family Memoir, p. 39.
> Hyde Genealogy, Vol. I, pp. 246-55.
> Bodge's Soldiers in King Philip's War.

State No.                                        Society No.

## 24     ORLANDO ELMER CLARK.     2175

Born November 9, 1850, in Darien, Genesee Co., N. Y.

Generation.          Line of Descent from John Clark.
6  Rufus Clark (1820-1893) Eunice A. Wheeler (1821———).
5  Ezra Clark (1783-1832) Cinderella Carter (1796-1879).
4  Paul Clark (1750-1804) Sarah Wheeler (———).
3  John Clark[2] (1719———) Elizabeth Williams (———).
2  Nathaniel Clark (1694-1772) Mary Vrenner (1690-1754).
1  John Clark[1] (1655-1736) Rebecca Beaumont (———).

JOHN CLARK[1] of Saybrook, Ct. Appointed Lieutenant at Fort Saybrook, 1693. Commissioned by Gov. Robert Treat. Lieut. of Train Band, commissioned by Gov. Winthrop, 1699. Commissioned Captain by Gov. Winthrop, 1702. Later as Major of the Train Band, commanded the troops to protect the library of Yale College at the time of its removal from Saybrook to New Haven in 1718.

> Colonial Records of Connecticut.
> Original Commissions and orders in possession of Mr. Orlando Elmer Clark.

### (Supplemental.)

### LINE OF DESCENT FROM JOHN DRURY.

Generation.

7  Rufus Clark (1820-1893) Eunice A. Wheeler (1821——).
6  Jacob Wheeler (1782-1831) Hannah Drury (1786-1843).
5  Ebenezer Drury (1743-1808) Miriam Goodale (1748——).
4  Zedekiah Drury (1716-1777) Hannah Wooley (1716——).
3  Caleb Drury (1683-1723) Elizabeth Eames (1685——).
2  Thomas Drury (1668-1723) Rachael Rice (1664——).
1  John Drury (1646-1678) Mary Shrimpton (——).

JOHN DRURY.[1] Was Lieutenant in King Philip's War in 1675.

> Bodge's Soldiers in King Philip's War.
> Blood's History of Temple, N. H.
> Turner's Genealogy of Humphrey Turner.
> Vinton's Richardson Memorial.

State No.                                              Society No.

## 25          ROBERT CAMP.          2281

### Born June 1, 1859, in Milwaukee, Wis.

Generation.          Line of Descent from Nathan Gold.

7  Hoel Hinman Camp (1822——) Caroline Rebecca Baylies (1825-1859).
6  Horatio Nelson Baylies (1800-1849) Rebecca Bradley (——).

5  Nicholas Baylies (1768-1847) Mary Ripley (1778-1830).
4  Silvanus Ripley (1749-1787) Abigail Wheelock (——1818).
3  Eleazar Wheelock (1711-1779) Sarah Davenport Maltby (——).
2  John Davenport (1669-1731) Martha Gold Selleck (——1712).
1  Nathan Gold (——1694) Martha Harvey (1620-1694).

## MAJOR NATHAN GOLD.[1]  Assistant, 1657, 1662 and 1694. Major 1666. Member of Committee of Defense against the Dutch, 1662. Representative to the First Colonial Congress in New York, 1690. Major of Dragoons, 1675.

> Register Society Colonial Wars, 1896.
> Camp Monograph.
> History of Bridgewater, Mass.
> History of Medfield.

### (Supplemental.)

### LINE OF DESCENT FROM ELEAZAR WHEELOCK.

Generation.

7  Hoel Hinman Camp (1822——) Caroline Rebecca Baylies (1825-1859).
6  Horatio Nelson Baylies (1800-1849) Rebecca Bradley (——).
5  Nicholas Baylies (1768-1847) Mary Ripley (1778-1830).
4  Silvanus Ripley (1749-1787) Abigail Wheelock (——1818).
3  Eleazar Wheelock (1711-1779) Sarah Davenport Maltby (——).
2  Ralph Wheelock (1683——) Ruth Huntington (1682——).
1  Eleazar Wheelock (1654-1731) Elizabeth Fuller (——1689).

ELEAZAR WHEELOCK[1] of Medfield, Mass. "Commanded a corps of cavalry and was very successful in repelling the irruptions of the Indians in the new settlements. During the Indian wars his house in Mendon was converted into a garrison to which the settlers resorted for safety. It was several times besieged."

> Memoirs of Rev. Eleazar Wheelock, D.D., first President of Dartmouth College, Sec. I, p. 12.
> Tilden's History of Medfield, pp. 506-508.
> Mendon Records.

(Supplemental.)

## LINE OF DESCENT FROM GOV. WILLIAM BRADFORD.

Generation.

8  Hoel Hinman Camp (1822———) Caroline Rebecca Baylies (1825-1859).

7  David Manning Camp (1788-1871) Sarepta Savage (1793-1852).

6  Abel Camp, Jr., (1756-1839) Anna Manning (1762-1830).

5  David Manning (1726-1807) Anna Hamilton (———).

4  Samuel Manning (———) Irene Ripley (1700———).

3  Joshua Ripley (———1739) Hannah Bradford (1662-1738).

2  William Bradford[2] (1624-1704) Alice Richards (1627-1671).

1  William Bradford[1] (1588-1657) Alice Carpenter (1590-1670).

WILLIAM BRADFORD[2] was, next to Miles Standish, chief military man of the Plymouth Colony. In King Philip's War was Commander-in-Chief of the Plymouth Forces. At Narragansett Fort Fight received a musket ball in his flesh, which he carried the remainder of his life. In that encounter both parties fought for their very existence; nearly 1,000 Indians fell and about 150 of the English were killed or wounded. In the war with the Indians had the rank of Major, was Assistant Treasurer and Deputy Governor of Plymouth from 1682 to 1686, and from 1689 to 1691. In 1691 was one of the Council of Massachusetts.

> Dow's Plymouth, p. 38.
> Ripley Genealogy.
> Manning Genealogy (now in manuscript).
> New England Hist. and Gen. Register.
> Merton's Memorials.
> Bodge's Soldiers in King Philip's War.
> Register Society Colonial Wars.
> Larned's History of Windham.
> Camp Monograph.
> Sharon Country Church and Town Registers.

WILLIAM BRADFORD.[1]  Governor of Plymouth Colony 1621, 1632, 1637, 1639, 1643, 1648, 1656.

> Palfrey's History of New England, Vol. I, p. 408.
> Bancroft's History United States, Vol. I, pp. 210-211.
> Colonial Records.
> Bodge's Soldiers in King Philip's War, p. 455.

State No.                                          Society No.

# 26        RICHARD CARPENTER.        2282

Born Aug. 3, 1858, in Oberlin, Ohio.

Generation.        Line of Descent from John Greene.

7  Franklin Carpenter (1831——) Helen M. Roberts (1831——).
6  Richard Carpenter (1789-1863) Elizabeth Austin (1799-1860).
5  Barlow Carpenter (1747-1819) Sarah Goss (——).
4  Oliver Carpenter (1716——) Martha Greene (1722——).
3  Barlow Greene (1695——) Lydia Harding (——).
2  Peter Greene (1655-1723) Elizabeth Arnold (1659-1728).
1  John Greene (1620-1708) Ann Almy (1627-1709).


JOHN GREENE[1] of Warwick, R. I.  Attorney General,
1657-1660. Assistant, 1660-1690. Deputy, 1664-1680.
Major, 1683-86. Member of Gov. Andros' Council, 1686.
Deputy Governor, 1690-1700.

> Austin's Genealogical Dictionary of Rhode Island, p. 88.
> Colonial Records.


State No.                                          Society No.

# 27        THOMAS EDWARD CAMP.        2283

Born August 1, 1865, in Milwaukee, Wis.

Generation.        Line of Descent from Thomas Benedict.

8  Hoel Hinman Camp (1822——) Anna Searle (1833——).
7  Thomas Bigelow (1801-1882) Janet C. Gordon (1811-1891).
6  Thomas Bigelow (1769-1843) Mary Griffith (1771-1835).
5  Hopestill Bigelow (1731——) Esther Benedict (——)
4  Samuel Benedict (——) —————— —————— (——).
3  Thomas Benedict (1679-1714) Elizabeth Barnum (——).
2  Samuel Benedict (——1719) Rebecca Andrews (——).
1  Thomas Benedict (1617-1690) Mary Bridgum (1618-1717).

THOMAS BENEDICT[1] of Norwalk, Ct.   Commissioned
Lieutenant in Capt. Bryan Newton's foot company, at Jamaica,
1665.   Member of Colonial Assembly at Hemstead.   Deputy
from Norwalk to General Court, 1670 and 1675.

> Register Society Colonial Wars, 1896, pp. 74-284.
> Book of Deeds in office of Secretary of State, N. Y., Vol.
>     II, p. 26.
> Camp Monograph.
> Bigelow Genealogy.
> Benedict Genealogy.

(Supplemental.)

### LINE OF DESCENT FROM JOHN BIGELOW.

Generation.

7   Hoel Hinman Camp (1822——) Anna Searle Bigelow (1833——).
6   Thomas Bigelow[2] (1801-1882) Janet C. Gordon (1811-1891).
5   Thomas Bigelow[1] (1769-1843) Mary Griffith (1771-1835).
4   Hopestill Bigelow (1731——) Esther Benedict) (————).
3   Ebenezer Bigelow (1698——) Hannah Browne (————).
2   Joshua Bigelow (1655-1745) Elizabeth Flagg (1657-1729).
1   John Bigelow (1617-1703) Mary Warren (——1691).

JOHN BIGELOW.[1]   Soldier in Pequot War in 1637.   Soldier in
King Philip's War, 1676.

> Register Society Colonial Wars, 1896.
> G. B. Howe's Bigelow Genealogy.
> Bodge's Soldiers in King Philip's War, pp. 170-171-272-
>     286-376-418.

(Supplemental.)

### LINE OF DESCENT FROM WILLIAM BRADFORD.

Generation.

8   Hoel Hinman Camp (1822——) Anna Searle Bigelow (1833——).
7   David Manning Camp (1788-1871) Serepta Savage (1793-1852).
6   Abel Camp, Jr. (1756-1839) Anna Manning (1762-1830).
5   David Manning (1726-1807) Anna Hamilton (————).
4   Samuel Manning (————) Irene Ripley (1700——).
3   Joshua Ripley (——1739) Hannah Bradford (1662-1738).
2   William Bradford[2] (1624-1704) Alice Richards (1627-1671).
1   William Bradford[1] (1588-1657) Alice Carpenter (1590-1670).

WILLIAM BRADFORD.[1]  Governor of Plymouth Colony 1621, 1632, 1637, 1639, 1643, 1648, 1656.

> Palfrey's History of New England, Vol. I, p. 408.
> Bancroft's History United States, Vol. I, pp. 210-211.
> Colonial Records.
> Bodge's Soldiers in King Philip's War, p. 455.

State No.                                                    Society No.

## 28          EDWARD JOY PAUL.          2366

Born October 28, 1858, in Kenosha, Wis.

Generation.     Line of Descent from Abraham Fowler.

6  George Howard Paul (1826-1890) Pamela Susan Joy (1836——).
5  Nehemiah Horton Joy (1809-1868) Pamela Susan Parmalee (1806-1879).
4  Josiah Parmalee (1773-1841) Pamela Fowler (1778-1835).
3  Caleb Fowler (1727-1807) Anna Rose (1735-1798).
2  Josiah Fowler (1688-1757) Hannah Baldwin (————).
1  Abraham Fowler (1652-1720) Elizabeth Bartlett (——1742).

ABRAHAM FOWLER[1] of Guilford, Ct.  Deputy to General Court, 1697, 1698, 1699, 1701, 1702 and 1703, et seq.  Assistant, 1713 to 1720.  Judge of County Court and of the Higher Court of Chancery Jurisdiction.  Sergeant in King Philip's War and wounded in "The Great Swamp Fight."

> "William Fowler, the Magistrate, and one line of His Descendants," 1867.
> Connecticut Colonial Records.

(Supplemental.)

### LINE OF DESCENT FROM JONATHAN MARSH.

Generation.

7  George Howard Paul (1826-1890) Pamela Susan Joy (1836——).
6  Nehemiah Horton Joy (1809-1868) Pamela Susan Parmalee (1806-1879).
5  Abiathar Joy (1788-1813) Fanea Horton (1790-1852).

4 Nehemiah Horton (————) Phila Marsh (1760-1850).
3 William Marsh (1732-1780) Rachel Coates (1735-1780).
2 Jonathan Marsh (1699-1749) Esther Osborn (1705-1749).
1 Jonathan Marsh (1672 after 1731) Mary ———— (1668-9-1731).

JONATHAN MARSH[1] was in the Indian fight at Haverhill.
Wounded at Haverhill Ferry on August 29, 1708.

> Chase's History of Haverhill, p. 217.
> John Marsh, of Salem, His Descendants, by Col. Lucius
> B. Marsh, Revised by Rev. Dwight W. Marsh, 1888,
> p. 25.
> Account of James Richardson Marsh, in Munsell's Am.
> Ancestry, Vol. III, p. 138.
> Historical Collections of Essex Institute, Vol. I (1859),
> p. 116.
> Account of Geo. H. Paul, Munsell's Am. Ancestry,
> Vol. IV, p. 231.
> Joy's Thomas Joy and His Descendants, 1900, pp. 81
> and 100.

(Supplemental.)

LINE OF DESCENT FROM NATHANIEL HIBBARD.

Generation.

6 George Howard Paul (1826-1890) Pamela Susan Joy (1836———).
5 Amos Paul (1793-1835) Mary Ann Choate (1800-1843).
4 James Paul (1768-1809) Elethear Jewett (1770-1822).
3 Daniel Jewett (1744-1829) Zelpha Hibbard (1745-1829).
2 Zebulon Hibbard (1714-1788) Hannah Barr (1711-1759).
1 Nathaniel Hibbard (1680-1725) Sarah Crane (1680-1721).

NATHANIAL HIBBARD,[1] Sergeant. From the Colonial Records,
May 12, 1712, we learn "additional wages voted to Nathanial Hibbard of
Windham as Corporal, 4s 4d, a soldier in late Expedition against Canada."

> Genealogy of the Hibbard Family, by Augustine George
> Hibbard of Woodstock, Conn., Hartford, 1901, p.
> 26.
> Munsell's Am. Ancestry, Vol. IV, p. 231. Ancestry of
> George Howard Paul.
> Hibbard Genealogy, 1901, pp. 66 (No. 279), 37 (No.
> 103), 26 (No. 36).
> John Marsh of Salem and His Descendants, pp. 7, 8, 25,
> 36, 38, 75.

WILLIAM MARSH[8] was one of the officers and men in the Colonial Service from the town of Fulton, Mass., between 1755-1761, during the French War.

> John Marsh of Salem and His Descendants, p. 76.
> Benedict Tracy's History of Sutton, p. 779.

### (Supplemental.)

## LINE OF DESCENT FROM JOHN GALLOP.

Generation.

10  George Howard Paul (1826-1890) Pamela Susan Joy (1836———).
9   Nehemiah Horton Joy (1809-1868) Pamela Susan Parmalee (1806-1879).
8   Abiathar Joy (1788-1813) Fanea Horton (1790———).
7   Jesse Joy (1759-1821) (unknown).
6   David Joy (1724-1809) Elizabeth Allen (1724-1820).
5   David Joy (1693-4-1739) Ruth Ford (————).
4   Joseph Joy (1668-1716) Elizabeth Andrews (1665-1743).
3   Joseph Joy (1645-1697) Mary Prince (1649-1726).
2   Thomas Joy (1611-1678) Joan Gallop (———1691).
1   John Gallop (———1650) Christabel ——— (———1655).

DAVID JOY[6] served in the French and Indian War and was at the taking of Fort Ticonderoga in 1775.

> Joy's Thomas Joy and His Descendants, New York, 1900, pp. 74, 81 and 100.

JOHN GALLOP'S[1] trading shallop was the principal means of communication between the Massachusetts Bay Colony and the settlements on Narragansett Bay and Long Island Sound. In July, 1636, attacked murderers of friend, John Oldham, off Block Island, with help of two young sons, and one other man, dispatched or captured 14 Indians. Served in campaign that grew out of this incident.

> Joy's Thomas Joy and His Descendants, 1900, pp. 11-12.
> Gallup's Genealogy of Gallup Family, 1893, pp. 18-245.
> Drake's History of Boston, pp. 198, 33-66-67-70-74-81-100.
> Joy Family Record.
> Joy's Thomas Joy and His Descendants.

(Supplemental.)

Generation.      Line of Descent from John Hathaway.

7  George Howard Paul (1826-1890) Pamela Susan Joy (1836———).
6  Amos Paul (1793-1835) Mary Ann Choate (1800-1843).
5  James Paul (1768———) Elethear Jewett (1770-1822).
4  James Paul (1725-1814) Sarah White (1729———).
3  John White (1683-1748) Elizabeth Hathaway (169— -1741).
2  Ephraim Hathaway (1661-1716) Elizabeth (———) (———).
1  John Hathaway, Sr. (1629-1704-5) Ruth (———) (———).


JOHN HATHAWAY, Sr.[1] and his son, Ephraim Hathaway, both
served in the war against the French in 1690, known as King William's
War.

> Collections of Old Colony Historical Society of Taunton,
> Mass., Vol VI, printed 1899. Article entitled The
> Early Hathaways in Taunton, p. 80.
> Genealogy of Paul Family.
> Descendants of William Paul of Colony of Plymouth,
> by E. J. Paul, in manuscript.
> Records of Bristol County, Mass., Probate Office, Register
> of Deeds Office and records of the Towns and
> Churches of Taunton and Dighton.


JAMES PAUL[4] served as member of Col. Bagley's Regiment on the
Expedition to Louisburg in 1759, according to the diary of Jacob Haskins,
who enlisted April 6, 1759, in his Majesty's service for the reduction of
Canada. He parted with his friends April 16th and marched as far as
Mr. Kingman's tavern in Easton, the same day, and to Mr. Bent's tavern
in Milton, April 17, 1759; arrived at Castle William April 18, arrived at
the Shearley April 19, was turned over to Captain Glover in Col. Bagley's
Regiment, slept that night in a cold meeting house without blankets, passed
muster and embarked on board the "Wolfe," May 8. Sailed for Louisburg,
May 15; arrived there May 24, disembarked May 27, 1759; embarked on
board the transport "Squirrel" for Boston, Dec. 2, 1761, according to his
own diary. This diary is now, in 1899, in the possession of Ruth Ann
Low, residing at the old Burt homestead, Berkley, Mass., and contains
this entry, "Oct. 9, 1759, James Paul got his discharge from the regiment."

> James E. Seaver, Secretary of the Old Colony Historical
> Society at Taunton, Mass., has no doubts concerning
> this diary.

(Supplemental.)

### LINE OF DESCENT FROM THOMAS LOW.

Generation.
7   George Howard Paul (1826-1890) Pamela Susan Joy (1836———).
6   Amos Paul (1793-1835) Mary Ann Choate (1800-1843).
5   Jacob Choate (1773-1818) Rosamond Parmalee (1771-1853).
4   Isaac Choate (1734-1813) Elizabeth Low (1736-1817).
3   Jonathan Low (1708-1761) Sarah Perkins (1711-1761).
2   Jonathan Low (1665-1749) Mary Thompson (————).
1   Thomas Low (————) Martha Boardman (——1720).

THOMAS LOW.[1]  Soldier in King Philip's War; received by reason of that fact, a "right" in Narragansett No. 1 (now Buxton, Me.), which was afterwards sold by his son Jonathan Low, in consideration of "love, good will and affection" and 500 pounds, and support during natural life, to his son Jonathan Low, Jr., and conveyed by deed dated Aug. 26, 1749. Acknowledged Aug. 30, 1749. Recorded Oct. 26, 1749, in Essex deeds, Salem, Vol. 90, p. 55.

> Rev. Anson Titus of Tuft's College, Mass., Genealogist, is authority for this reference.
> Bodge's Soldiers in King Philip's War, p. 415.

State No.                                          Society No.

## 29          HOWARD GREENE.          2367

Born May 17, 1864, in Milwaukee, Wis.

Generation.      Line of Descent from John Howland.
9   Thomas Arnold Green (1827-1894) Elizabeth Lynes Cadle (1831-1892).
8   Welcome Arnold Greene (1795-1870) Sarah Gardner (1807-1833).
7   Zenas Gardner (1769-1848) Susanah Hussey (1771-1842).
6   George Hussey (1738-1804) Deborah Paddock (1739-1815).
5   Daniel Paddock (1707-1743) Susanah Gorham (1705-1777).
4   Stephen Gorham (1683-1743) Elizabeth Gardner (——1763).
3   John Gorham (1652-1716) Mary Otis (1654-1732).
2   John Gorham (1621-1676) Desire Howland (1623-1683).
1   John Howland (1592-1673) and Elizabeth Tilley (1607-1687).

JOHN GORHAM[2] of Plymouth, Mass. Captain of a Plymouth Troop in the war with the Narragansett Indians, 1675. Lieutenant in the war with the Dutch, 1673. Died of a fever contracted during the Narragansett War.

> Austin's Ancestral Dictionary of Rhode Island, p. 110.
> Austin's One Hundred and Sixty Allied Families, p. 22.
> Bodge's Soldiers in King Philip's War.

COL. JOHN GORHAM.[3] Was in the Great Swamp Fight, 1675. In the Canadian Expedition, 1690. Second in command under Col. Benjamin Church in the expedition of 1704.

> Register Society Colonial Wars, 1896.

JOHN HOWLAND.[1] Sept. 6, 1620, sailed from England in the Mayflower. Thirteenth signer of the Mayflower compact. Soldier under Capt. Miles Standish in the "First Encounter," Dec. 6, 1620. Assistant to Governors Winslow and Prence, 1633-1635. Placed in command of the trading fort on the Kennebec River in 1634. Deputy many years.

> Register Society Colonial Wars, 1896.
> Austin's One Hundred and Sixty Allied Families, pp. 137-138-139.

State No.                                              Society No.

30      FRANK GORDON BIGELOW.      2400

Born Sept. 28, 1847, in Hartford, N. Y.

Generation.      Line of Descent from John Bigelow.

6  Dr. Thomas Bigelow (1801-1882) Janet C. Gordon (1811-1891).
5  Thomas Bigelow (1769-1843) Mary Griffith (1771-1835).
4  Rev. Hopestill Bigelow (1731——) Esther Benedict (————).
3  Ebenezer Bigelow (1696——) Hannah Brown (————).
2  Joshua Bigelow (1655-1745) Elizabeth Flagg (1657-1729).
1  John Bigelow (1617-1703) Mary Warren (——1691).

JOHN BIGELOW² of Watertown, Mass.  Soldier in the
Pequot War in 1637.

Register Society Colonial Wars, 1896, p. 285.
Howe's Bigelow Genealogy.
Bodge's Soldiers in King Philip's War, pp. 170-171-272-
286-376-418.

State No.                                    Society No.

## 31          WILLIAM BIGELOW.          2401

Born Dec. 17, 1851, in Hartford, N. Y.

Generation.      Line of Descent from John Bigelow.

6  Dr. Thomas Bigelow (1801-1882) Janet C. Gordon (1811-1891).
5  Thomas Bigelow (1769-1843) Mary Griffith (1771-1835).
4  Rev. Hopestill Bigelow (1731——) Esther Benedict (————).
3  Ebenezer Bigelow (1698——) Hannah Brown (————).
2  Joshua Bigelow (1655-1745) Elizabeth Flagg (1657-1729).
1  John Bigelow (1617-1703) Mary Warren (——1691).

JOHN BIGELOW² of Watertown, Mass.  Soldier in the
Pequot War in 1637.

Register Society Colonial Wars, 1896, p. 285.
Howe's Bigelow Genealogy.
Bodge's Soldiers in King Philip's War, pp. 170-171-272-
286-376-418.

State No.                                    Society No.

## 32          *HENRY CLAY PAYNE.          2402

Born November 23, 1843, in Ashfield, Mass.

Generation.      Line of Descent from Moses Paine.

7  Orrin P. Payne (————) Eliza Ames (————).
6  Samuel Payne (————) Laura Elmer (————).
5  Joseph Ruggles Paine (1735-1825) ———— (————).
4  Samuel Paine (1689——) Susanna Ruggles (1702——).
3  Stephen Paine, Jr. (1652-1690) Ellen Veasey (————).
2  Stephen Paine (1628-1691) Hannah Bass (————).
1  Moses Paine (——1643) Elizabeth ———— (————).

*Deceased

STEPHEN PAINE[2] of Braintree, Mass. Sergeant in the "Ancient and Honorable Artillery Company" in 1649. Served under Capt. Thomas Prentice in the Mount Hope Campaign, King Philip's War. Also under Lieutenant Edward Oakes. Also in Capt. Poole's Company.

Paine Genealbgy, 1880, p. 165.
Bodge's Soldiers in King Philip's War, pp. 81-91-260.

MOSES PAINE.[1] Contributed largely toward paying the expenses of the earlier Indian wars.

Paine Genealogy, 1880, p. 165.
Bodge's Soldiers in King Philip's War.

State No.                                                          Society No.

33        CHARLES LOUIS JONES.        2403

Born January 17, 1872, in Milwaukee, Wis.

Generation.        Line of Descent from Joseph Judson.

8  Charles P. Jones (1835——) Louise Van Dyke (1837——).
7  Richard Van Dyke (1815-1876) Mary Ware Thomas (1816——).
6  Richard Van Dyke (——1856) Lydia Wood (1782-1837).
5  Rev. Henry Van Dyke (1744-1804) Huldah Lewis (1746-1806).
4  David Lewis (1711-1783) Phoebe Curtis (1713——).
3  James Lewis (1679-1766) Hannah Judson (1681-1756).
2  James Judson (1649-1721) Rebecca Welles (1655-1717).
1  Joseph Judson (1619-1690) Sarah Porter (1626-1696).

JOSEPH JUDSON[1] of Stratford, Ct. Ensign of the Stratford Train Band. Lieutenant in 1672 and served in King Philip's War. In 1665 appointed by the General Court one of a commission to defend the coast, from Stratford to Rye, against a threatened invasion by the Dutch. Deputy to General Court 1659-1667.

Orcutt's History of Stratford, pp. 110-197-196-200-250.
Connecticut Colonial Records, Vols. I and II, pp. 21, 181.
Bodge's Soldiers in King Philip's War, p. 468.
Register Society Colonial Wars, 1896.

(Supplemental.)

## LINE OF DESCENT FROM THOMAS WELLES.

Generation.

9  Charles P. Jones (1834——) Louise Van Dyke (1837——).
8  Richard Van Dyke (1810-1876) Mary Ware Thomas (1816——).
7  Richard Van Dyke (1775-1856) Lydia Wood (1782-1837).
6  Henry Van Dyke (1744-1804) Huldah Lewis (1746-1806).
5  David Lewis (1711-1783) Phoebe Curtis (1713——).
4  James Lewis (1679-1766) Hannah Judson (1681-1756).
3  James Judson (1649-1721) Rebecca Welles (1655-1717).
2  Thomas Welles, Jr. (1627-1682) Hannah Tuttle (1633——).
1  Thomas Welles (1598-1660) Elizabeth Hunt (——1640).


THOMAS WELLES.¹  Governor from 1655 to 1658; Magistrate,
1637-1660; Deputy Governor, 1654; Commissioner of Colonies, 1649.


JAMES LEWIS.⁴  Representative for over seven years; Lieutenant,
1714; Captain 2d Company, 1714; Ensign, 1709.

> Savage's Genealogical Dictionary, Vol. II, pp. 575-1229-
> 1237; Vol. IV, p. 479.
> Register Society Colonial Wars, pp. 303-694.
> Colonial Records, Hartford.
> Orcutt's Stratford, pp. 1229-1230-1237-1238-1325-1350.
> Goodwin's Genealogical Notes.
> Seabury's Centenary.
> Records in Adjutant General's office, Hartford, Conn.


State No.                                                    Society No.

## 34     *BEDFORD BROWN HOPKINS.   2404

Born October 16, 1834, in Clarence, N. Y.

Generation.     Line of Descent from John Bigelow.

6  Otis Ransom Hopkins (1780-1846) Lavinia Spoor (1799-1852).
5  Ichabod Hopkins (1744-1819) Sarah Bigelow (1744——).
4  Asa Bigelow (1720-1754) Dorothy Otis (1721-1794).
3  John Bigelow (1681-1770) Sarah Bigelow (——1754).
2  Joshua Bigelow (1655-1745) Elizabeth Flagg (1657-1729).
1  John Bigelow (1617-1703) Mary Warren (——1691).

*Deceased

JOSHUA BIGELOW.[3]  Soldier in King Philip's War, in Capt. Nathaniel Davenport's Company.  Was severely wounded.  Received grant of land for his services.

> Register Society Colonial Wars, 1896, p. 285.
> Howe's Bigelow Genealogy.
> Bodge's Soldiers in King Philip's War, pp. 170-171-272-286, etc.

JOHN BIGELOW[1] of Watertown, Mass.  Soldier in Pequot War in 1637.  Soldier in King Philip's War in 1676.

State No.                                           Society No.

## 35     ARTHUR NYE McGEOCH.     2405

Born April 19, 1869, in Milwaukee, Wis.

Generation.     Line of Descent from Richard Treat.

- 10  Peter McGeoch (1833-1895) Catherine Ellen Harvey (1835-1885).
- 9  Enoch Dole Harvey (1811-1888) Mary Hubbard Nye (1812-1859).
- 8  Asahel Hubbard Nye (1790-1861) Mary Andrews (1789-1812).
- 7  Elijah Nye (1766-1852) Mary Hubbard (1765-1838).
- 6  Eleazer Hubbard (1722-1812) Abigail Hollister (1735-1819).
- 5  Thomas Hollister (1707-1784) Abigail Talcott (1717-1812).
- 4  Thomas Hollister (1672-1741) Dorothy Hills (1677-1741).
- 3  John Hollister (1644-1711) Sarah Goodrich (1649-1700).
- 2  John Hollister (1612-1665) Joanna Treat (1618-1694).
- 1  Richard Treat (1584-1669) Alice Gaylord (1594——).

RICHARD TREAT.[1]  Deputy.  Assistant, 1657-1665. Named in the Royal Charter.  One of the Patentees of Connecticut.

> Connecticut Colonial Records, Vol. I, pp. 103-124-138-149-163, etc.
> Treat Genealogy, p. 28.
> Register Society Colonial Wars, 1896, p. 402.
> Savage's Genealogical Dictionary, pp. 483-484.
> Bond's Watertown, pp. 795-796.
> Descendants of Geo. Hubbard, p. 8.
> American Ancestry.

State No.                                    Society No.

## 36        RICHARD BENBRIDGE        2406
### WETHERILL.

Born January 10, 1859, in La Fayette, Ind.

Generation.       Line of Descent from Jacob Morgan.

5  Charles Mayer Wetherill (1824-1871) Mary C. Benbridge (1833-
   ——).
4  Charles Wetherill (1798-1838) Margretta S. Mayer (1804-1882).
3  Samuel Wetherill (1764-1829) Rachel Price (1766-1844).
2  John Price (————) Rebecca Morgan (————).
1  Jacob Morgan (1716-1793) Rachel Pearsall (————).

JACOB MORGAN.[1]  Served in French and Indian War
in 1754-55-56-57.  Captain in 1755, in the First Battalion of
Pennsylvania Troops.  Captain in the Second Battalion in the
Expedition which captured Fort Duquesne in 1758.  Commission dated 1755.  Was Adjutant in 1760.

Pennsylvania Archives, second series, Vol. II, pp. 533-
516-539-545-559-608.

State No.                                    Society No.

## 37    DR. NATHANIEL A. GRAY.    2487

Born March 8, 1842, in Chautauqua Co., N. Y.

Generation.       Line of Descent from John Gray.

5  Dr. Alfred William Gray (1802-1873) Valeria Elizabeth Dodd.
4  Judge John Gray (1769-1859) Diantha Burritt (1755——).
3  John Gray (1739-1822) Elizabeth Skeel (1745-1824).
2  John Gray (1707-1761) Anne Hebbard (1706-1746).
1  John Gray (1680-1711) Ruth Hebbard (1683——).

JOHN GRAY[2] of Sharon, Mass.  Served in Capt.
Ephraim Williams' Company, and in Capt. Isaac Wyman's
Company at Fort Massachusetts, 1754-55.

Massachusetts Archives, Military series, Vol. 93, pp.
155-173.

State No.                                    Society No.

## 38          BEN RUSSELL ROGERS.          2500

Born October 26, 1874, in Calumet, Mich.

Generation.      Line of descent from Thomas Howes.

8  Horace Brewster Rogers (1837——) Mary Frances Russell (1844-
   ——).
7  Samuel Russell (1813-1879) Sarah Crane Smith (1820-1887).
6  John Keyzar Smith (1785-1855) Catharine McDonald (1795-
   1881).
5  Abraham Smith (1754-1808) Sarah Crane (1757-1829).
4  Colonel Thaddeus Crane (1728-1803) Sarah Paddock (——1773).
3  Peter Paddock (1697-1760) Sarah Howes (1695-1776).
2  Jonathan Howes (1669-1750) Sarah ——— (———).
1  Thomas Howes (——1676) Sarah Bangs (———).


THOMAS HOWES.[1]  Ensign at Yarmouth, Mass.,
1672-74.  Made Captain June 3, 1674.  Member of War
Council, 1667.

> Plymouth Colony Records, Vol. V, pp. 92, 113, 143,
> 146, 164.
> Bodge's Soldiers in King Philip's War.
> List of Prominent Officers of Plymouth and Yarmouth
> Colonies.


State No.                                    Society No.

## 39          PAUL DENISON SEXTON.          2501

Born May 11, 1866, in Milwaukee, Wis.

Generation.      Line of Descent from George Denison.

7  Joseph Kellogg Sexton (1805-1881) Mary Esther Taylor (1832-
   ——).
6  Anson Hawley Taylor (1800-1864) Esther Denison (1800-1869).
5  Henry Denison (1753-1836) Mary Gallup (——1843).
4  Daniel Denison (1721-1776) Esther Wheeler (1722-1814).
3  Daniel Denison (1680-1747) Mary Stanton (1687-1724).
2  John Denison (1646-1698) Phebe Lay (1650-1699).
1  George Denison (1618-1694) Ann Borrodell (1615-1712).

GEORGE DENISON.[1]  Served under Major John Mason and Major Talcott.  Chosen with Major John Mason to assist the Pequot Chiefs, to govern their tribe.  Captain of New London County forces in King Philip's War.  Second in command under Major Robert Treat in the Great Swamp Fight.  Captured the Indian Chief Canonchet.  Assistant and Deputy from Stonington to the General Court, 15 terms.

> Register Society Colonial Wars, 1896, p. 309.
> Baldwin & Clift's "Captain George Denison," pp. 6, 17, 120, 131, 163, 165.

State No.                                    Society No.

## 40    ALONZO GILBERT SEXTON.    2502

Born March 26, 1836, in Somers, Connecticut.

Generation.     Line of Descent from Jonathan Kellogg.

4  Joseph Kellogg Sexton (1805-1881) Lucy Amelia Billings (1811-1845).
3  Stephen Sexton (1771-1832) Lucy Kellogg (1777-1857).
2  Joseph Kellogg (1742——) Lucy Warner (————).
1  Jonathan Kellogg (1721-1745) ———— (————).

JONATHAN KELLOGG.[1]  Captain in the 1st Massachusetts Regiment, in the expedition against Louisburg in 1745.

> New England Hist. and Gen. Register, Vol. XXIV, 369.

State No.                                    Society No.

## 41    ARTHUR TAYLOR SEXTON.    2608

Born August 22, 1860, at Milwaukee, Wis.

Generation.     Line of Descent from George Denison.

7  Kellogg Sexton (1805-1881) Mary Esther Taylor (1832——).
6  Anson Hawley Taylor (1800-1864) Esther Denison (1800-1869).
5  Henry Denison (1753-1836) Mary Gallup (——1843).

4  Daniel Denison² (1721-1776) Esther Wheeler (1722-1814).
3  Daniel Denison¹ (1680-1747) Mary Stanton (1687-1724).
2  John Denison (1646-1798) Phebe Lay (1650-1699).
1  George Denison (1618-1694) Ann Borrodell (1615-1712).

GEORGE DENISON.¹  Captain in New London County forces in King Philip's War.  Served under Major John Mann and Major Talcott.  Second in command to Major Robert Treat in Great Swamp Fight.  Served on the frontier. Captured the Indian Chief Canonchet.  Chosen with Major John Mason to assist the Pequot Chiefs to govern their tribes. Assistant and Deputy from Stonington to the General Court, 15 terms.

Register Society Colonial Wars, 1896, p. 309.
Baldwin & Clift's "Captain George Denison," Worcester,
1881, pp. 6, 17, 120, 131, 163, 165.

State No.                                                              Society No.

42      BENJAMIN WILSON SMITH.      2792

Born January 19, 1830, in Harrison Co., W. Va.

Generation.      Line of Descent from David Wilson.
5  Abel Timothy Smith (1803-1875) Deborah Spencer Wilson (1806-1871).
4  Benjamin Wilson (1747-1827) Phoebe Davisson (1777-1849).
3  William Wilson (1722-1801) Elizabeth Blackburn (1725-1806).
2  David Wilson² (————) ———— (————).
1  David Wilson¹ (————) ———— (————).

BENJAMIN WILSON⁴ of Virginia.  Was in 1774 attached to the right wing of the Dunmore army as a lieutenant and marched against the old Chillicothe Indian towns on the Scioto.  While negotiations were going on with the Indians at Camp Charlotte, was near village of Westfall, Pickaway Co., Ohio.  Lieutenant Wilson served as aide to Lord (Governor) Dunmore, Commander-in-Chief.  Rendered valuable service in the campaign and a competent and reliable authority declares that he acquired, by zeal and attention to duty, the confidence of his superior officers.

American Historical Record, June, 1873, pp. 263-4-5.
Drake's Life of Tecumseh, p. 46.
Wither's Chronicles of Border Warfare, p. 136.
Palmer's Calendar Virginia State Papers.
Haymond's History of Randolph County, W. Va.

State No.                                                    Society No.

## 43  WILLIAM STEVENS BROCKWAY.  2858

Born December 29, 1855, in Ripon, Wis.

Generation.          Line of Descent from John Lyman.

8  Edward Payson Brockway (1832——) Susan Maria McKnight 1833——).
7  Thomas McKnight (1786-1836) Harriet Clapp (1798-1883).
6  Joseph Clapp (1764-1839) Susannah Lyman (1770-1842).
5  Timothy Lyman (1744-1815) Dorothy Kinney (1752-1829).
4  Elias Lyman (1715-1803) Anne Phelps (——1791).
3  Moses Lyman (1689-1762) Mindwell Sheldon (——1780).
2  Moses Lyman (1662-1701) Anne ——— (———).
1  John Lyman (1623-1698) Dorcas Plumb (———).

JOHN LYMAN.[1]  Born in High Onger, County Essex, England, Sept., 1623.  Came to New England with his father, Richard; married Dorcas, daughter of John Plumb, of Branford, Conn.  Settled in Northampton, Mass., in 1654, where he resided until his death, Aug. 20, 1690.  Lieutenant, served in the famous Falls fight, above Deerfield, May 18, 1676.

Wight's The Wights, p. 120.
McKnight Family Circle, p. 27.
The Lyman Family.
Register Society Colonial Wars, 1898-1899.

(Supplemental.)

## LINE OF DESCENT FROM HUMPHREY ATHERTON.

Generation.

8  Edward Payson Brockway (1832———) Susan McKnight (1833-
———).
7  Picket Brockway (1788-1833) Nancy Stevens (1799-1874).
6  Abner Brockway (1754-1808) Catharine Marvin (1756-1831).
5  Elisha Marvin (1717-1801) Catharine Mather (1717-1799).
4  Timothy Mather (1681-1755 Sarah ——— (——1756).
3  Richard Mather (1653-1688) ——— (———).
2  Timothy Mather (1628——) Katherine Atherton (———).
1  Humphrey Atherton (——1661) ——— (———).


HUMPHREY ATHERTON.[1]  Deputy, 1638 et seq.  Speaker,
1653.  Governor's Assistant, 1654-1661.  Lieutenant, 1645.  Captain of
Militia, 1646, and of the Ancient and Honorable Artillery Company,
1650-1658.  Commanded Expedition against the Narragansetts, 1656.
Major General, 1661.

Register Society Colonial Wars, 1897-1898, p. 416.


(Supplemental.)

## LINE OF DESCENT FROM THOMAS TRACY.

Generation.

7  Edward Payson Brockway (1832——) Susan McKnight (1833-
———).
6  Picket Brockway (1788-1833) Nancy Stevens (1799-1874).
5  Abner Brockway (1754-1808) Catharine Marvin (1756-1831).
4  Elisha Marvin (1717-1801) Catharine Mather (1717-1799).
3  Reinold Marvin (1669-1737) Martha Waterman (1680-1753).
2  Thomas Waterman (1644-1708) Miriam Tracy (1646——).
1  Thomas Tracy (1610-1685) ——— (———).


THOMAS TRACY.[1]  Ensign 1st Company Militia, Connecticut,
1666.  Lieutenant, 1672, of New London Co. Dragoons, enlisted to fight
the Dutch and Indians.  Member of General Court 27 sessions.  Commissary King Philip's War.  Commissioner, 1678 et seq.

Register Society Colonial Wars, 1897-1898, p. 561.

State No.                                                      Society No.

## 44        *HAROLD GREEN UNDER-        2859
WOOD.

Born August 1, 1852, in Litchfield, N. Y.

Generation.        Line of Descent from Philip Smith.

7  John De Loss Underwood (1817-1855) Marcia Dening Green
   (1827——).
6  Beriah Green (1795-1874) Daraxa Foote (1797-1885).
5  Freeman Foote (1759-1842) Silence Clark (1763-1832).
4  Daniel Foote (1724-1801) Martha Stillman (1726-1794).
3  John Stillman (1693-1775) Mary Wolcott (1695-1777).
2  George Stillman (1654-1728) Rebecca Smith (1668-1750).
1  Philip Smith (1634-1684) Rebecca Foote (1634-1701).


PHILIP SMITH.¹  Born in Wethersfield, Conn., in
1634.  Moved to Hadley, Mass., in 1659.  Was commissioned and served as "Lieutenant of the Troop" in Hadley,
Mass., as recorded in the "Record Book of the Hadley Hopkins
School," of which school he was one of the committee.  He was
a member of the General Court of Massachusetts and also a
Justice in the County Court.

> Record Book of the Hadley Hopkins School of Hadley,
> Mass.
> Goodwin's The Foote Family, or The Descendants of
> Nathaniel Foote, Hartford, 1849.


State No.                                                      Society No.

## 45    WILLIAM MATTOCKS FARR.   2860

Born November 23, 1853, in Peachum, Va.

Generation.        Line of Descent from James Trowbridge.

7  Asahel Farr (1820-1887) Martha Jackson Wheeler (1828-1878).
6  Alpheus Farr (1784-1852) Sibyl Farr (1787-1843).
5  Asahel Farr (1766——) Lydia Snow (1772——).

*Deceased.

4   Zerubbazel Snow (1742——) Mary Trowbridge (1745——).
3   James Trowbridge (1717——) Jerusha Park (1722——).
2   William Trowbridge (1684——) Sarah Ward (————).
1   James Trowbridge (1636-1717) Margaret Jackson (————).

## JAMES TROWBRIDGE[1] of Newton, Mass. Deputy to General Court from Cambridge, 1700-03. Served in King Philip's War. Lieutenant, 1675.

Register Society Colonial Wars, 1897-1898, p. 563.

(Supplemental.)

### LINE OF DESCENT FROM JONATHAN FARR.

Generation.
4   Asahel Farr (1820-1887) Martha Jackson Wheeler (1828-1878).
3   Alpheus Farr (1784-1852) Sybbell Farr (1787-1843).
2   Asahel Farr (1766——) Lydia Snow (1772——).
1   Jonathan Farr (1757-1800) Mercy Winslow (1736——).

History of Hardrich, p. 266. Colonial Wars.

State No.                                             Society No.

## 46        WILLIAM JAMES HENRY        2876
## STRONG.

Born October 16, 1869, in Council Bluffs, Ia.

Generation.        Line of Descent from Anthony Hawkins.
7   William Barstow Strong (1837——) Abby Jane Moore (1839-
——).
6   Elijah Gridley Strong (1803-1859) Sarah Ashley Partridge (1806-
1865).
5   Elisha Strong (1718-1794) Sarah Lewis (1726——).
4   Daniel Lewis (1681——) Mary Strong (1692-1759).
3   Asahel Strong (1668-1739) Margaret Hart (——1735).
2   Thomas Hart (1644-1726) Ruth Hawkins (1649-1724).
1   Anthony Hawkins (——1674) ———— (————).

## ANTHONY HAWKINS.[1] Was Governor's Assistant.

Public Records of Connecticut, 1665-1677, pp. 31, 93,
146, 159, 191.
Hollister's History of Connecticut, Vol. I, p. 531.

Farmer's First Settlers in New England, p. 139.
Savage's Genealogical Dictionary, Vol. II, pp. 367, 382;
    Vol. III, p. 89.
Cheney Family.
American Ancestry, Vol. X, p. 95.
Strong Genealogy, Vol. I, pp. 282, 283; Vol. II, pp.
    1272, 1271, 1270, 1264.
Stephen Hart and His Descendants.


(Supplemental.)

## LINE OF DESCENT FROM THOMAS WELLES.

Generation.
9  William Barstow Strong (1837——) Abby Jane Moore (1839-
    ——).
8  Elijah Gridley Strong (1803-1859) Sarah Ashley Partridge (1806-
    1865).
7  Elijah Strong (1762-1838) Sylvia Gridley (1769-1813).
6  Deacon Timothy Gridley (1743-1827) Rhoda Woodruff (1746-
    1817).
5  Timothy Gridley (1711-1764) Esther Porter (——1762).
4  Thomas Gridley (——1758) Hannah Wilcockson (1685-1733).
3  Samuel Gridley (1647-1712) Esther Thomson (1655——).
2  Thomas Thomson (————) Ann Welles (————).
1  Thomas Welles (——1660) ———— (————).


THOMAS WELLES.[1]  Deputy Governor of Connecticut, 1654-56-
57-59. Governor, 1655-58.

             Bodge's Soldiers in King Philip's War, Appendix, pp.
                464-465.
             Connecticut Public Records, 1635-1665.


State No.                              Society No.

## 47    WILLIAM STARK SMITH.    2877

Born July 31, 1871, in Utica, N. Y.

Generation.    Line of Descent from Aaron Stark.

7  William Belinger Smith (1827——) Sarah Jane Stark (1832——).
6  Jedediah Lathrop Stark (1793-1862) Hannah Gager (1799-1882).
5  Joshua Stark (1761-1819) Olive Lathrop (1764-1825).

4 Abial Stark (1724-1770) Chloe Hinckley (———1828).
3 Abial Stark (—————) Mary Walworth (—————).
2 Aaron Stark (1654——) Mehitable Shaw (—————).
1 Aaron Stark (1602-1685) ——————— (—————).

## AARON STARK.[1] Soldier in the Pequot and King Philip's War.

> See affidavit made by him on the 11th of June, 1673, is in the archives of the Town of Westerly, R. I.
>
> Walworth's Walworths of America.
>
> Bodge's Soldiers in King Philip's War.
>
> Walworth's Hyde Genealogy, Vol. I, pp. 248-253.
>
> Enrollment list of soldiers in "The Late Narragansett War," containing the name of said Aaron Stark, said list being certified to in Town Clerk's office of Valuntown, December 23, 1860, by Elisha Potter, Town Clerk.

State No.                                   Society No.

## 48      RALPH PERCY PERRY.      2940

### Born June 22, 1859, in Reedsburg, Wis.

Generation.      Line of Descent from Henry Short.

6 Oliver H. Perry·(1820-1886) Mary J. McCloud (1827——).
5 John McCloud (1787-1836) Polly Brown (1789-1847).
4 Noah Brown (1752-1821) Judith Short (1751-1822).
3 Ebenezer Short (1721——) Abigail Balcom (—————).
2 Matthew Short (1688-1731) Margaret Freeman (—————).
1 Henry Short (1652-1706) Sarah Whipple (———1691).

## MATTHEW SHORT.[2] Chaplain in the service of the Colony of Massachusetts.

> Folsom's History of Saco and Biddeford, Me.
>
> W. L. Chaffin's History of Eaton, Mass.
>
> Massachusetts State Papers, Archives, Vol. VI and VII.
>
> Redlon's Saco Valley Settlements and Families.
>
> Owen's "Old Times in Saco."
>
> Daggett's History of Attleboro.

State No.                                                    Society No.

## 49     FRANCIS JEWETT JOHNSON.     2941

Born May 2, 1876, in Saugatuck, Mich.

### LINE OF DESCENT FROM JOHN BOYNTON.

Generation.

7  Otis Russell Johnson (1815-1895) Emily Wells (————).
6  Moses Johnson (1787-1822) Philomela Jewett (————1839).
5  Samuel Johnson (1748-1814) Susannah Searle (1750————).
4  Samuel Johnson (1699-1773) Rachel Boynton (————1799).
3  Ichabod Boynton (1677————) Elizabeth Hazeltin (1683————).
2  John Boynton (1647-1719) Hannah Keyes (1654-1719).
1  John Boynton (1614-1670) Ellen Pell (————).


JOHN BOYNTON.¹  At the time the expedition against Narragansett was organized, he joined the company of Capt. Joseph Gardiner of Ipswich, Mass., and was one of the ninety-five men of this company mustered with the army commanded by Major Samuel Appleton, at Dedham Plain, Dec. 9, 1675.  The Massachusetts Council proclaimed to the soldiers mustered on Dedham Plain, that if they played the man, took the Fort and drove the enemy out of Narragansett County, which was their great seat, that they should have a gratuity of land besides their wages.  John Boynton was a soldier grantee from Bradford, Mass., of Narragansett township No. 3, Sowhegan West, now Amherst, N. H., his son, Ichabod Boynton, being claimant about 1743.


(Supplemental.)

### LINE OF DESCENT FROM RICHARD WICOM.

Generation.

7  Otis Russell Johnson (1815-1895) Emily Wells (1833————).
6  Moses Johnson (1787-1822) Philomela Jewett (————1839).
5  Samuel Johnson (1748-1814) Susannah Searle (1750————).

4  Samuel Johnson (1699-1773) Rachel Boynton (——1799).
3  Samuel Johnson (1671-1753) Francis Wicom (1675-1750).
2  Daniel Wicom (1635-1700) Mary Smith (——1690-1).
1  Richard Wicom (——1663-4) Ann ——— (——1674).

DANIEL WICOM.² Captain of the Military Company and a leading man in town affairs in Rowley, Mass. Appointed and served on committee for making divisional town lines, 1685. A member of the General Court, 1689 and 1699. A member of Captain Nicholas Paige's troop which accompanied Major Thomas Savage in the Expedition to Mount Hope, August 23, 1675. Quartermaster, June 24, 1676. His name appears in the "Credits" of Captain John Whipple of Ipswich, Mass. His name appears in list of soldier grantees of Narragansett township No. 4, now Greenwich, Mass.

(Supplemental.)

### LINE OF DESCENT FROM JOHN JOHNSON.

Generation.

6  Otis Russell Johnson (1815-1895) Emily Wells (1833-1901).
5  Moses Johnson (1787-1822) Philomela Jewett (——1839).
4  Samuel Johnson (1748-1814) Susannah Searle (1750——).
3  Samuel Johnson (1699-1773) Rachael Boynton (——1799).
2  Samuel Johnson (1671-1753) Frances Wicom (1675-1750).
1  John Johnson (1630-1685) Hannah Crosby (1634-1717).

JOHN JOHNSON.¹ At the commencement of King Philip's War (1675), Captain John Johnson, Ensign in the Essex Regiment, commanded by Major Daniel Dennison. Participated in the battles of this war. Killed in the defense of Sudbury, Mass., April 21, 1676. That his services as a soldier and ensign in the Essex Regiment were appreciated is shown by the following record taken from the records of the Colony of Massachusetts Bay in New England, Vol. 5 (1674-1686), p. 172; pub. 1854, viz.: "1677, 22d October, John Johnson, Captain; Thos. Tenney, Ens., at Rowley." "The Military Company at Rowley being destitute of a captain, this Court doth hereby order Ensign John Johnson to be captain and Sergeant Thos. Tenny to be his ensign, to the foot company there and they have their commission accordingly."

> Savage's Genealogical Dictionary, Vol. II, pp. 554-5.
> Bodge's Soldiers in King Philip's War, p. 474.
> Gage's History of Rowley, Mass., pp. 146, 360 and 446.
> Blodgett's Early Settlers of Rowley, pp. 127-13.

(Supplemental.)

## LINE OF DESCENT FROM THOMAS WELLS.

Generation.

9  Otis Russell Johnson (1815-1895) Emily Wells (1833——).
8  Andrew Shelton Wells (1800——) Mary Warner (1805——).
7  David Wells (1774-1855) Abigail Shelton (1775-1852).
6  David Wells (1738-1790) Johannah Willcoxson (1741-1800).
5  David Wells (1699-1742) Mary Thompson (1706——).
4  John Wells (1675-6-1734) Mary Judson (1679-1743).
3  John Wells, Jr. (1648-1713) Mary Hollister (————).
2  John Wells (1621-1660) Elizabeth Bourne (————).
1  Thomas Wells (1598-1660) Elizabeth Hunt (————).

THOMAS WELLS.[1] Settled at Hartford, Conn., in the summer of 1636. Next year was chosen Magistrate by the planters; was in active participation in the duties of this office during the Pequot War in 1637. This office he held until his decease in 1659-60. In 1639 was chosen the first treasurer of the colony under the new constitution, and variously continued in this office until 1651, at which time on account of other duties, he asked to be eased of the treasurer's place and the request was granted. In 1641 was chosen secretary of the colony and held the office in subsequent years. In 1649 he was one of the commissioners of the "United Colonies." In 1654 Governor Hopkins, being in England, and Deputy Governor Haynes having died, he was elected by the whole body of freemen, convened at Hartford, moderator of the General Court, and this year was again appointed one of the commissioners of the United Colonies, but other duties prevented him from serving and this year he was also chosen Deputy Governor; in 1655 Governor and in 1656 and 1657, Deputy Governor; in 1658 again Governor and in 1659 again Deputy Governor.

Trumbull's History of Connecticut, etc., 1818, Vol. I, pp. 64, 67, etc.

Trumbull's History of Connecticut, 1898, Vol. 1, pp. 83, 87, 144, 177, 179, 184.

Hoodley's Records of New Haven, Conn., 1858, 2 Vols., pp. 80, 170 and 490.

Walker's History First Churches in Hartford, 1884, 1663, 1883, pp. 130, 167, 419.

Historical Catalogue of First Church in Hartford, 1633-1883, p. 10, 1885.

Porter's Historical Notices of Connecticut, p. 22, 1842.

Paige's History of Cambridge, Mass., 1877, pp. 30, 589, 653.

Savage's Genealogical Dictionary, Vol. IV, p. 478.

State No.                                    Society No.

50              HORATIO GATES.              3069

Born November 12, 1853, in Brooklyn, N. Y.

LINE OF DESCENT FROM TIMOTHY DWIGHT.

Generation.
7   Perez Dickinson Gates (1818-1864) Louise Huges (1834——).
6   Horatio Gates (1784-1840) Electa Dickinson (1790-1823).
5   Thomas Asa Gates (1751-1820) Margaret Dwight (1758-1841).
4   Elihu Dwight (1737-1760) Penelope Graves (1733-1785).
3   Nathaniel Dwight (1712-1784) Hannah Lyman (1709-1794).
2   Nathaniel Dwight (1666-1711) Mehitable Partridge (1675——).
1   Timothy Dwight (1629-1718) Anna Flynt (————————).

TIMOTHY DWIGHT.[1]   Cornet of Horse and Captain of Foot.   Served in ten Indian expeditions.   Deputy to the General Court of Massachusetts.

Register General Society Colonial Wars, 1896, p. 313.
Dwight Genealogy, Vol. I, pp. 449-450 and see pp. ante.
Gates Genealogy.
Graves Genealogy.
Lyman Genealogy.
Talcot's New York and New England Families.

State No.                                    Society No.

51    CHARLES HERMAN RUGGLES.   3159

Born December 31, 1870, in Omaha, Neb.

Generation.       Line of Descent from Cadwallader Colden.

5   Geo. D. Ruggles (1833——) Alma Hammond L'Hommedieu
        (1843——).
4   David Ruggles (1783-1837) Sarah Colden (1791-1849).
3   David Colden (1760-1798) Gertrude Wyncoop (1767-1790).
2   Cadwallader Colden (1724-1797) Elizabeth Ellison (1726-1815).
1   Cadwallader Colden (1688-1776) Alice Christie (————————).

CADWALLADER COLDEN.[1] Lieutenant Governor
of New York Colony from 1761 until 1775.

> History of Ruggles Family, Mass., 3d Ed., 1896, pp. 154, 155, 156 and 157.
>
> History of Ruggles Family, privately printed, in possession of applicant.
>
> Colden—Correspondence of Cadwallader Colden, Esq., of New York, with his cousin, Cadwallader Colden, of Hamilton, Scotland, in 1796; Colden Family Bible, and records in possession of General George David Ruggles.

State No.                                          Society No.

## 52    THOMAS LATHROP KENNAN.    3160

Born February 22, 1827, in Morristown, N. Y.

Generation.    Line of Descent from William Brewster.

9  George Kennan (1795-1876) Mary Tullar (1801-1866).
8  Rev. Thomas Kennan (1773-1853) Sally Lathrop (1775-1831).
7  Denison Lathrop (1755——) Sarah Harris (1757-1852).
6  George Harris (1720——) Sarah Hubbard (1735——).
5  Gibson Harris (1694-1761) Phoebe Denison (1697——).
4  George Denison (1671-1720) Mary Wetherell (1668-1711).
3  Daniel Wetherell (1630-1719) Grace Brewster (1639-1717).
2  Jonathan Brewster (1593-1659) Lucretia Oldham (——1678).
1  William Brewster (1560-1643) Mary Love (1562-1627).

WILLIAM BREWSTER.[1]    Drafted the Mayflower
compact.   Member and Chaplain of the first military company
organized at Plymouth under Captain Miles Standish.   Served
against the Indians.

Register Society Colonial Wars, 1897-8, p. 430.

(Supplemental.)

LINE OF DESCENT FROM JONATHAN BREWSTER.

Generation.

8  George Kennan (1795-1876) Mary Tullar (1801-1866).
7  Rev. Thomas Kennan (1773-1853) Sally Lathrop (1775-1831).
6  Denison Lathrop (1755——) Sarah Harris (1757-1852).

5  George Harris (1720———) Sarah Hubbard (1735———).
4  Gibson Harris (1694-1761) Phoebe Denison (1697———).
3  George Denison (1671-1720) Mary Wetherell (1668-1711).
2  Daniel Wetherell (1630-1719) Grace Brewster (1639-1711).
1  Jonathan Brewster (1593-1659) Lucretia Oldham (———1678).


DANIEL WETHERELL.² Captain and Commissary in charge of New London depot of supplies in King Philip's War. In the years 1675-6 Capt. Daniel Wetherell lived at New London; helped raise an army to go against the Indians. In the winter of 1675-6 an army of one thousand men was raised. In May the General Court at New London authorized the enlistment of 350 men as a standing army. These forces, which were under command of Major Talcott, were almost immediately ordered into the field. Mr. Wetherell and Mr. Douglas were the commissaries and New London the depot for supplies. Capt. George Denison had command of the company raised in New London.

History of New London, pp. 185-363.
Register Society Colonial Wars, 1897-8, p. 75.


JONATHAN BREWSTER.¹ Was Representative from Duxbury, 1639-41-42-44. Member of Capt. Miles Standish's Duxbury Company. Military Commissioner in Pequot War.

Register Society Colonial Wars, 1897-8, p. 430.


(Supplemental.)

LINE OF DESCENT FROM GEORGE DENISON.

Generation.
8  George Kennan (1795-1876) Mary Tullar (1801-1866).
7  Rev. Thomas Kennan (1773-1853) Sally Lathrop (1775-1831).
6  Denison Lathrop (1755———) Sarah Harris (1757-1852).
5  George Harris (1720———) Sarah Hubbard (1735———).
4  Gibson Harris (1694-1761) Phoebe Denison (1697———).
3  George Denison (1671-1720) Mary Wetherell (1668-1711).
2  John B. Denison (1648-1698) Phoebe Lay (1650-1699).
1  George Denison (1619-1694) Ann Borodell (———————).


JOHN DENISON.² Soldier in King Philip's War and served first, under Capt. Thomas Lathrop in 1675; was in the fight at Muddy Brook, where nearly all the members of the company were killed, including Capt. Thomas Lathrop. After that he served under Major Appleton and was wounded in the fight at Indian Fort on the 19th of December, 1675.

Bodge's Soldiers in King Philip's War, pp. 138-156. '

GEORGE DENISON.[1] Received commission as Lieutenant in October, 1736, at Stonington. Appointed Commissioner for the County of New London in March, 1703. Was Deputy of the General Court in October, 1671. Appointed a Commissioner of Deputy for Stonington, Sept. 3, 1689, and again May 11, 1693, and in 1694. Commissioned Captain of Volunteers, September, 1689. Captain of New London Co. forces in King Philip's War under Major Mann and Major Talcott. Second in command to Major Treat in the Great Swamp Fight. Captured Indian Chief Canonchet. Chosen with Major Mason to assist the Pequot Chief to govern their tribes. He is said to have been the most conspicuous soldier of New London County, and distinguished himself in King Philip's War as a skillful and enterprising commander.

Vol. VIII, Colonial Records, p. 58.
Vol. IV, Colonial Records, pp. 5 and 458.
History of New London, pp. 185-186 and 188.
History of Stonington, pp. 336-337.
Savage's Genealogical Dictionary, Vol. II, p. 36.

State No.                                                    Society No.

# 53   ALBERT KELLOGG STEBBINS.   3161

Born June 21, 1875, in Milwaukee, Wis.

Generation.    Line of Descent from Rowland Stebbins.

8  Lemuel Dibble Stebbins (1841——) Georgia Anna Green (1846-——).
7  Albert Burt Stebbins (1812-1881) Mary Jeannette Beebe (1813-1870).
6  Lamar Stebbins (1774-1861) Deborah Stebbins (1778-1865).
5  Edward Stebbins (1729-1816) Elizabeth Burt (1741-1821).
4  John Stebbins (1690-1743) Sarah Warriner (1690-1715).
3  Joseph Stebbins (1652-1721) Sarah Dorchester (1653-1746).
2  Thomas Stebbins (1620-1683) Hannah Wright (——1660).
1  Rowland Stebbins (1594-1671) Sarah —— (1591-1649).

THOMAS STEBBINS.[2]  Was with Capt. Wm. Turner at the Falls Fight, May 18, 1676.

> Bodge's Soldiers in King Philip's War, p. 251.
> Sheldon's History of Deerfield, p. 160.
> Records of National Society Colonial Wars in the Matters of Douglas Merritt and Arthur C. Thomson.
> Sheldon's History of Deerfield, Vol. II, (gen.), p. 316.
> New England Hist. and Gen. Reg., Vol. XXXVIII, p. 157.
> Savage's Genealogical Dictionary.

(Supplemental.)

### LINE OF DESCENT FROM SAMUEL SMITH.

Generation.

8   Lemuel Dibble Stebbins (1841——) Georgia Anna Green (1846-——).

7   Albert Burt Stebbins (1812-1881) Mary Jeannette Beebe (1813-1870).

6   Lamar Stebbins (1774-1861) Deborah Stebbins (1778-1865).

5   Lemuel Stebbins (1737-1808) Rhoda Wait (1766——).

4   John Stebbins (1692-1741) Deborah Lamb (1731——).

3   Edward Stebbins (1656-1712) Sarah Graves (1679——).

2   John Graves (——1677) Mary Smith (1630-1668).

1   Samuel Smith (1602-1680) Elizabeth ——— (1602-1686).

SAMUEL SMITH.[1]  Came from Ipswich on the "Elizabeth," April 30, 1634. Removed to Hadley in 1659. A leading man in the settlement and as Lieutenant was in charge of military affairs until 1678.

> Sheldon's History of Deerfield, pp. 310, 175 and 176.
> Field Genealogy, p. 210.
> Savage's Genealogical Dictionary. "Graves" and "Smith."

(Supplemental.)

### LINE OF DESCENT FROM HENRY SHERMAN.

Generation.

11   Lemuel Dibble Stebbins (1841——) Georgia Anna Green (1846-——).

10   Albert Burt Stebbins (1812-1881) Mary Jeannette Beebe (1813-1870).

9   James Beebe (1781-1875) Polly Ward (1790-1860).

8  Lemuel Beebe (1743-1813) Hannah Dibble (1745-1825).
7  Lemuel Beebe (————) Lydia Taylor (————).
6  James Beebe (1681——) Abigail Sherman (1688-1708).
5  Samuel Sherman (1641-1700) Mary Letterton (————).
4  Samuel Sherman (1618-1684) Mary Mitchell (————).
3  Edmond Sherman (————) Judith Angiers (————).
2  Henry Sherman (————) Susan Hills (————).
1  Henry Sherman (——1589) Agnes ———— (——1580).


SAMUEL SHERMAN.[4]  Second named freeman of Stratford, Conn.
(now Bridgeport).  Executive officer with plenary powers in procuring
the Union of New Haven, Milford, Branford, Guilford and Stamford
under the Crown Charter.  For many years assistant to the Governor of
Connecticut.

> Trumbull's Colonial Records of Connecticut, 425, 426,
> 436, 437, Vol. I; 13, 21, 521, Vol. II.
> New Haven Colonial Records (1663-5), 549.
> The Sherman Family, by Rev. David Sherman, p. 24.
> New England Hist. and Gen. Reg., pp. 63-69.
> Rev. Thomas Roberts' Century Sermon, delivered Jan.
> 1st, 1801, republished in Danbury News, March 12-
> 26, 1879.
> Hinman's Early Puritan Settlers of Connecticut, p. 172.


State No.                                              Society No.

## 54   GERRY WHITING HAZLETON.  ——

### Born February 24, 1829, in Chester, N. H.

Generation.        Line of Descent from John Pike.

7  William Hazleton (1789-1864) Mercy Janet Cochrane (1798-
1884).
6  John Hazleton (1736-1815) Hannah Chase (1754-1826).
5  Johnson Chase (1730-1761) Abigail Pike (1729-1804).
4  Thomas Pike (1700-1757) Lois Perley (1702——).
3  Joseph Pike (1674-1757) Hannah Smith (1675——).
2  Joseph Pike (1638-1694) Susanna Kingsbury (——1710).
1  John Pike (1614-1698) Mary ———— (————).


JOHN PIKE.[1]  "1639 all men of Newbury were divided
into four companies for defense, of which one was commanded

by John Pike." Thereafter for some years he is mentioned in the records as lieutenant. Removed to Woodbridge, 1667; elected President of Woodbridge, 1671; chosen one of Gov. Carterat's Council. Member of Supreme Court by virtue of being a justice of the peace.

> 1670, "Gov. Carterat to Mr. John Pike, Justice of the Peace and President of the Court at Woodbridge ＊ ＊ ＊ Greeting." New Jersey Archives, Vol. I, p. 63.
> Roll of Officers of Militia elected and sworn in for Woodbridge, 1673, includes John Pike, Captain. N. J. Archives, Vol. I, p. 134.
> Register Society Colonial Wars, 1899-1902, p. 732.
> Genealogical Register, 1902, Index Pike, p. 732.
> Coffin's Newbury.

(Supplemental.)

### LINE OF DESCENT FROM JAMES SMITH.

Generation.
6  William Hazleton (1789-1864) Mercy Janet Cochrane (1798-1884).
5  John Hazleton (1736-1815) Hannah Chase (1754-1826).
4  Johnson Chase (1730——) Abigail Pike (1729-1804).
3  Thomas Pike (1700-1761) Lois Perley (1702——).
2  Joseph Pike 2d (1674-1757) Hannah Smith (1675——).
1  James Smith (1645-1690) Sarah Coker (1643——).


JAMES SMITH[2] of Newbury, Mass. Lieutenant in the crusade of Phipps against Quebec, on return from which, in October, 1690, he perished by shipwreck on Anticosti. Capt. Stephen Greenleaf, Lieut. James Smith, Ens. Wm. ————, Sergt. Increase Pillsbury, Jabez Musgrave and four more were cast away and drowned at Cape Breton. Inventory of estate of Lieut. James Smith, who deceased Nov. 1, 1690, being cast-away on Cape Breton on the Canada Expedition, taken March 23, 1691.

> Essex Co. Hist. Collection, Vol. V.
> Coffin's Newbury, p. 155.
> Register Society Colonial Wars, 1892, p. 763.

State No.                                    Society No.

## 55    OLIVER FREDERIC DWIGHT.   3508

Born March 13, 1866, in Martin, Mich.

Generation.      Line of Descent from John Dwight.

7  Corydon G. Dwight (1828——) Sarah Elizabeth Northrup (1833-1876).
6  Samuel Dwight, Jr. (1800——) Darsa Bartlett (1807-1868).
5  Samuel Dwight (1765-1817) Ruth Furnace (1763-1853).
4  Simeon Dwight (1719-1776) Sibyll Dwight (1725-1784).
3  Henry Dwight (1676-1732) Lydia Hawley (1680-1748).
2  Timothy Dwight (1629-1718) Anna Flynt (1643-1685).
1  John Dwight (————) Hannah ——— (————).

TIMOTHY DWIGHT.[2]  Cornet of Horse and Captain of Foot. Served in ten Indian campaigns. Was also Deputy to the General Court.

Dwight Genealogy, Vols. I and II.
Register Society of Colonial Wars, 1899-1902, p. 623.
Dr. Dwight's Descendants of John Dwight of Dedham, England.

State No.                                    Society No.

## 56   HARRY LAFAYETTE KELLOGG.  3532

Born June 24, 1872, in Madison, Wis.

Generation.      Line of Descent from Joseph Kellogg.

8  Clarence Kellogg (1844——) Julia Ann Adams (1848——).
7  La Fayette Kellogg (1819-1878) Rosa Ormsby Catlin (1824-1863).
6  Rowland Kellogg (1786-1826) Sarah Titus (1787-1868).
5  William Kellogg (1759-1824) Urania Bishop (————).
4  William Kellogg (1724——) Keziah Dewey (1726——).
3  Stephen Kellogg (1695-1738) Abigail Loomis (1701-1734).
2  Stephen Kellogg (1658-1722) Lydia Belden (1675-1759).
1  Joseph Kellogg (1626-1707) Abigail Terry (1646-1726).

JOSEPH KELLOGG.[1]  The County Court of Hadley, Mass., approved the choice of Joseph Kellogg as Sergeant of the Hadley Company or "Train Band," March, 1663. The General Court of Massachusetts appointed him 9 May, 1678, Ensign of the Foot Company in Hadley, and 7 October of the same year, Lieutenant in the same company. He was in command of the Hadley troops in the famous "Turners' Falls" fight, 18 May, 1676, which broke the power of the river tribes.

Bodge's Soldiers in King Philip's War.
Timothy Hopkins' The Kelloggs in the Old World and
    the New.
Savage's Genealogical Dictionary, Vol. III, p. 5.
The American Genealogical Record, Vol. II, Part One.
    Published in San Francisco, by Am. Gen. Record
    Publishers Co., 1897.
Foote Genealogy, p. 27.
Register Society Colonial Wars, 1899-1902, p. 685.

State No.                                        Society No.

## 57   CHARLES COPELAND RUSSELL.   3533

Born April 4, 1868, in Gouverneur, N. Y.

Generation.        Line of Descent from John Alden.

8  Cyrus H. Russell (1828-1875) Fannie Maria Copeland (1842-
    ——).
7  Clewley Copeland (1798-1878) Fanny Stowell (1812-1890).
6  Smith Copeland (1773-1854) Polly Wetherbee (1773-1853).
5  William Copeland (1730-1797) Mary Smith (——1786).
4  William Copeland (1695——) Mary Thayer (1689-1727).
3  William Copeland (1656-1716) Mary Bass (1669——).
2  John Bass (1632-1716) Ruth Alden (——1674).
1  John Alden (1599-1687) Priscilla Mullins (——1650).
        Register Society Colonial Wars, 1899-1902, p. 546.

State No.                                        Society No.

## 58      LEVI HORACE BANCROFT.    3558

Born December 26, 1860, in Sauk County, Wis.

Generation.      Line of Descent from Thomas Hurlbut.

8  George I. Bancroft (1835——) Helen M. Randolph (1842——).
7  P. J. Randolph (1809-1884) Alma J. Hurd (1817-1862).
6  Joseph J. Randolph (1774-1814) Eunice Hurlbut (1781-1837).

5  Rufus Hurlbut (——1781) Hannah Lester (————).
4  John Hurlbut (————) Mary Stoddard (————).
3  Stephen Hurlbut (1668——) Hannah Douglas (————).
2  Samuel Hurlbut (1644——) Mary ———— (————).
1  Thomas Hurlbut (1610——) Sarah ———— (————).

THOMAS HURLBUT.[1]  Soldier in 1635 under Lion Gardiner, who built and commanded the Fort at Saybrook, Connecticut. Served in the Indian wars. Particularly in the Pequot War, in which he was severely wounded. Was granted 120 acres of land by the Assembly on Oct. 12th, 1671, for services in the Indian wars.

> Hurlbut's Hurlbut Family Genealogy, pp. 15 to 18, 21, 28, 49 and 94.
> Family records in my possession bring the family history down to present time.
> Society Register, p. 677.
> Savage's Genealogical Dictionary, Vol. II, p. 506.
> Bodge's Soldiers in King Philip's War.

State No.                                    Society No.

59      HENRY ALVIN CROSBY.          ——

Born June 6, 1866, in Milwaukee, Wis.

Generation.      Line of Descent from Simon Crosby.

7  Francis James Crosby (1832——) Frances Adele Noyes (1837-——).
6  Frederic Crosby (1795——) Susanna Thaxter (————).
5  Michael Crosby (1771——) Asenath Blanchard (————).
4  Oliver Crosby (1744-1825) Rachel Stickney (————).
3  Oliver Crosby (1716-1746) Rebecca ———— (————).
2  Nathan Crosby (1674-1749) Sarah Shed (————).
1  Simon Crosby (1637-1725) Rachel Brackett (————).

> Register Society Colonial Wars, 1899-1902, p. 608.
> Savage's Genealogical Dictionary, pp. 476 and 477.
> Pope's Pioneers of Massachusetts, p. 124.
> Paige's History of Cambridge, 1630-1877, p. 519.
> Hazen's History of Billerica.

State No.                                    Society No.

60        OLIVER CLYDE FULLER.        ——

Born September 13, 1860, in Clarkesville, Ga.

Generation.        Line of Descent from John Sevier.

5   Henry Alexander Fuller (1835——) Martha Caroline Wyly (1840-
       1882).
4   Oliver Cromwell Wyly (1808-1893) Lucy Eddins (1812-1850).
3   James Rutherford Wyly (————) Sarah Hawkins Clark (————)
2   William Clark (————) Elizabeth Sevier (————).
1   John Sevier (1745-1815) Sarah Hawkins (————).


JOHN SEVIER.[1]  Settled in the Shenandoah Valley
when a young man and established there a village called New-
market.   This was a frontier line at the time and the Indians
were numerous and given to encroachment and young Sevier was
obliged to fight for his settlement.   He became celebrated
through his conflicts with the savages, conquering the neighboring
tribes in a number of engagements.   In 1772 he received the appointment of Captain in the Virginia line.   In the same year he
removed to Watauga, on the western slope of the Alleghanies.
In 1773 Lord Dunmore began war on the Indian tribes and
Sevier served through the campaign and distinquished himself at
the battle of Point Pleasant, October 10, 1774.   About the
beginning of the Revolutionary War, the citizens of Watauga
were desirous of being annexed to the Colony of North Carolina
and John Sevier drew up a memorial to the Legislature making
the request on the part of the citizens that they might so be annexed to the end that they might aid in the contest and bear their
full proportion of the expense of the war.

                National Encyc. of American Biography, Vol. III, p. 430,
                    1893.
                John H. Wheeler's Historical Sketches of North Carolina,
                    p. 449.
                John H. Wheeler's Reminiscences and Memoirs of North
                    Carolina, p. 462.

State No.                                                          Society No.

## 61   †JONATHAN FRANKLIN PEIRCE. ——

Born July 23, 1844, Utica, N. Y.

Generation.        Line of Descent from John Moulton.

5  Jonathan Lovering Peirce (1799-1875) Angelina Moulton (1810-1833).
4  Nathaniel Thayer Moulton (1787-1870) Lydia D. Holbrook (——1870).
3  Jonathan Moulton (1726-1787) Sarah Emery (1740-1817).
2  Jacob Moulton (1688-1751) Sarah Smith (——1695).
1  John Moulton (1638-1705) Lydia Taylor (1646-1729).

JOHN MOULTON.[1]  Elected Ensign March, 1690; was one of committee appointed to call out soldiers and attend to their equipment; served in King Philip's War, 1690. Representative September 12, 1692.

JACOB MOULTON.[2]  Sentinel under Captain Nicholas Gilman in a detachment at Gov. Hilton's garrison, July 3, 1710.

GENERAL JONATHAN MOULTON.[3]  Served under Capt. John Ladd, 1757.  Lieutenant Colonel 3d Regiment of Militia, 1760.

> Adjutant General's Report in Military History of New Hampshire, p. 31.
> Emery Genealogy, p. 42.
> History of Hampton, N. H., Vol. II, pp. 861, 863, 865.
> Some Descendants of John and William Moulton, p. 13 (1892).
> Dow's History of Hampton, N. H., Moulton Line, Vol. II, pp. 249-275, 278-9, 861.
> Register Society Colonial Wars, 1899-1902, pp. 239, 627, 628, 715.
> New Hampshire Colonial Papers, Vol. II, p. 71.
> Moulton Genealogy, p. 33.

†Life Member.

(Supplemental.)

LINE OF DESCENT FROM DR. ANTHONY EMERY.

Generation.

4   Jonathan Lovering Peirce (1799-1875) Angelina Moulton (1810-1883).

3   Nathaniel Thayer Moulton (1787-1870) Lydia D. Holbrook (——1870).

2   Jonathan Moulton (1726-1787) Sarah Emery (1740-1817).

1   Anthony Emery (1713-1781) Abigail Leavitt (1715-1799).

ANTHONY EMERY.[1]   Surgeon Louisburg Expedition, 1745. Served in Col. Blanchard's regiment at Crown Point in 1755. Commissioned Lieutenant under Captain John Moore.

Emery Genealogy, pp. 23-24.
Dow's History of Hampton, N. H., Vol. II.
Colonial Records, 1899-1902, pp. 627-628.

State No.                                                    Society No.

62      ALFRED WILLIAM GRAY.      ——

Born September 26, 1873, in Milwaukee, Wis.

Generation.        Line of Descent from John Gray.

7   Nathaniel A. Gray (1842——) Letitia Jane Dunn (1848——).

6   Alfred William Gray (1802-1873) Valeria Elizabeth Dodd (————).

5   John Gray (1769-1859) Diana Burrett (1775——).

4   John Gray (1739-1822) Elizabeth Steel (1745-1824).

3   John Gray (1707-1761) Anne Hebbard (1706-1746).

2   John Gray (1690-1711) Ruth Hebbard (1683——).

1   John Gray (————) ———— ———— (————).

JOHN GRAY.[1]   Served under Captain Ephraim Williams at Fort Massachusetts. Time of service, Oct. 14, 1754, to March 28, 1755. Served under Captain Isaac Wyman at Fort Massachusetts. Time of service, March 29, 1755, to June 16, 1755.

Massachusetts Archives, Military Series, Vol. XCIII, pp. 155-173.
Register Society Colonial Wars, 1899-1902, p. 649.
Gray Genealogy.

# List of Ancestors

BIGELOW, JOHN (1617-1703)

|  |  |
|---|---|
| Bigelow, Frank Gordon | 30 |
| Bigelow, William | 31 |
| Camp, Thomas Edward | 27 |
| Hopkins, Bedford Brown | 34 |

BIGELOW, JOSHUA (1655-1745)

|  |  |
|---|---|
| Hopkins, Bedford Brown | 34 |

BRADFORD, WILLIAM (1588-1657)

|  |  |
|---|---|
| Camp, Robert | 25 |
| Camp, Thomas Edward | 27 |
| Chapman, Chandler Pease | 4 |
| Strong, William Wolcott | 1 |

BRADFORD, WILLIAM (1624-1704)

|  |  |
|---|---|
| Strong, William Wolcott | 1 |

BREWSTER, WILLIAM (1560-1643)

|  |  |
|---|---|
| Kennan, Thomas Lathrop | 52 |

BREWSTER, JONATHAN (1593-1659)

|  |  |
|---|---|
| Kennan, Thomas Lathrop | 52 |

BUEL, JOHN (1671——)

|  |  |
|---|---|
| Kneeland, James | 10 |
| Flint, Wyman Kneeland | 6 |

BULKELEY, PETER (1643-1688)

|  |  |
|---|---|
| Swain, William Chester | 9 |

CHOATE, THOMAS (1671-1745)

|  |  |
|---|---|
| Paul, Edward Joy | 28 |

CLARK, JOHN (1655-1736)

|  |  |
|---|---|
| Clark, Orlando Elmer | 24 |

CLEMENT, ROBERT (1590-1658)

|  |  |
|---|---|
| Reade, Philip | 3 |

COFFIN, TRISTRAM (1605-1681)

|  |  |
|---|---|
| Coffin, William King | 11 |
| Usher, Ellis Baker | 8 |

COLDEN, CADWALLADER (1688-1776)

|  |  |
|---|---|
| Ruggles, Herman | 51 |

COOKE, FRANCIS (1583-1663)

|  |  |
|---|---|
| Reade, Philip | 3 |

CROSBY, SIMON (1637-1725)
|  |  |
|---|---|
| Crosby, Henry Alvin | 59 |

CRUTTENDEN, ABRAHAM (——1683)
|  |  |
|---|---|
| Paul, Edward Joy | 28 |

CURTIS, PHILIP (——1675)
|  |  |
|---|---|
| Flint, Wyman Kneeland | 6 |

DENISON, GEORGE (1618-1694)
|  |  |
|---|---|
| Sexton, Paul Denison | 39 |
| Sexton, Arthur Taylor | 41 |
| Kennan, Thomas Lathrop | 52 |

DRURY, JOHN (1646-1678)
|  |  |
|---|---|
| Clark, Orlando Elmer | 24 |

DWIGHT, TIMOTHY (1629-1718)
|  |  |
|---|---|
| Gates, Horatio | 50 |
| Dwight, Oliver Frederick | 55 |

EMERY, ANTHONY (1713-1781)
|  |  |
|---|---|
| Peirce, Jonathan Franklin | 61 |

FARR, JONATHAN (1757-1800)
|  |  |
|---|---|
| Farr, William Mattocks | 45 |

FARWELL, HENRY (——1670)
|  |  |
|---|---|
| Reade, Philip | 3 |

FITCH, THOMAS (1630-1690)
|  |  |
|---|---|
| Fitch, Grant | 13 |

FLINT, JOHN (——1686)
|  |  |
|---|---|
| Flint, Francis Gardiner | 22 |
| Flint, John Wyman | 19 |
| Flint, Wyman Kneeland | 6 |

FLINT, THOMAS (1603-1653)
|  |  |
|---|---|
| Flint, Wyman Kneeland | 6 |

FORD, WILLIAM (1633-1721)
|  |  |
|---|---|
| Paul, Edward Joy | 28 |

FOWLER, ABRAHAM (1652-1720)
|  |  |
|---|---|
| Paul, Edward Joy | 28 |

FULLER, MATTHEW (——1678)
|  |  |
|---|---|
| Flint, Wyman Kneeland | 6 |
| Kneeland, James | 10 |

GALLOP, JOHN (——1650)
Paul, Edward Joy                          28

GARDINER, LION (1599-1663)
Flint, Wyman Kneeland                      6

GOLD, NATHAN (——1694)
Camp, Robert                             25

GORHAM, JOHN (1621-1676)
Greene, Howard                           29

GORHAM, JOHN (1652-1716)
Greene, Howard                           29

GRAY, JOHN (1707-1781)
Gray, Nathaniel A.                       37
Gray, Alfred William                     62

GREENE, JOHN (1620-1708)
Carpenter, Richard                       26

GUILD, JOHN (——1682)
Underwood, Herbert Wight                 18

HALE, JOHN (1636-1700)
Swain, William Chester                    9

HATHAWAY, JOHN (1629-1705)
Paul, Edward Joy                         28

HAWKINS, ANTHONY (——1674)
Strong, William James Henry              46

HIBBARD, NATHANIEL (1680-1725)
Paul, Edward Joy                         28

HILDRETH, EPHRAIM (1680-1740)
Reade, Philip                             3

HILDRETH, RICHARD (1605-1693)
Reade, Philip                             3

HINMAN, EDWARD (——1681)
Flint, Wyman Kneeland                      6

HOWES, THOMAS (——1676)
Rogers, Ben Russell                      38

HOWLAND, JOHN (1592-1673)
Greene, Howard                           29
Swain, William Chester                    9

HURLBURT, THOMAS (1610——)
    Bancroft, Levi Horace    58

JOY, ABIATHAR (1788-1813)
    Paul, Edward Joy    28

JOY, DAVID (1724-1809)
    Paul, Edward Joy    28

JUDSON, JOSEPH (1619-1690)
    Jones, Charles Louis    33

KELLOGG, JONATHAN (1721-1745)
    Sexton, Alonzo Gilbert    40

KELLOGG, JOSEPH (1626-1707)
    Kellogg, Henry La Fayette    56

KNEELAND, EDWARD (1640——)
    Flint, Wyman Kneeland    6
    Kneeland, James    10

LANE, DANIEL (1740-1811)
    Usher, Ellis Baker    8

LANE, JOHN (———)
    Usher, Ellis Baker    8

LANE, JOHN (1701-1756)
    Usher, Ellis Baker    8

LATHROP, SAMUEL (——1700)
    Stark, Charles Gager    23

LAW, THOMAS (1632-1712)
    Paul, Edward Joy    28

LEWIS, JAMES (1679-1766)
    Jones, Charles Louis    33

LYMAN, JOHN (1623-1698)
    Brockway, William Stevens    43

MARSH, JONATHAN (1672-1731)
    Paul, Edward Joy    28

MARSH, WILLIAM (1732-1780)
    Paul, Edward Joy    28

MASON, THOMAS (1625-1676)
    Mason, William Lyman    17

MILLARD, ROBERT (——1662)
    Paul, Edward Joy    28

MINOTT, JAMES (1653-1735)
    Swain, William Chester    9

MORGAN, JACOB (1716-1793)
    Wetherell, Richard Benbridge    36

MOSELEY, JOHN (——1690)
    Wight, William Ward    7

MOULTON, JACOB (1688-1751)
    Peirce, Jonathan Franklin    61

MOULTON, JONATHAN (1726-1787)
    Peirce, Jonathan Franklin    61

NEWBERRY, BENJAMIN (——1703)
    Wight, William Ward    7

OAKES, EDWARD (1604-1689)
    Flint, Wyman Kneeland    6

PAINE, MOSES (——1643)
    Payne, Henry Clay    32

PAINE, STEPHEN (1628-1691)
    Payne, Henry Clay    32

PAUL, JAMES (1725-1814)
    Paul, Edward Joy    28

PERKINS, ISAAC (1650-1725)
    Paul, Edward Joy    28

PERKINS, JOHN (1590-1654)
    Reade, Philip    3
    Paul, Edward Joy    28

PERKINS, JOHN (1614-1686)
    Paul, Edward Joy    28

PHELPS, WILLIAM (1599-1672)
    Brown, Charles Curtis    14
    Simmons, Samuel Sweet    20

PIERSON, JOSEPH (————)
    Flint, Wyman Kneeland    6
    Kneeland, James    10

PIKE, JOHN (1614-1698)
                Hazleton, George Whiting          54

PRENTICE, THOMAS (1621-1710)
                Mason, William Lyman          17

READE, WILLIAM (1605-1663)
                Reade, Philip          3

READE, WILLIAM (1639-1706)
                Reade, Philip          3

READE, WILLIAM (1682-1753)
                Reade, Philip          3

READE, WILLIAM (1704-1773)
                Reade, Philip          3

READE, WILLIAM (1724-1769)
                Reade, Philip          3

SEVIER, JOHN (1745-1815)
                Fuller, Oliver Clyde          60

SHERMAN, SAMUEL (1618-1684)
                Stebbins, Albert Kellogg          53

SHORT, MATTHEW (1688-1731)
                Perry, Ralph Percy          48

SMITH, JAMES (1645-1690)
                Hazleton, George Whiting          54

SMITH, PHILIP (1634-1684)
                Underwood, Harold Greene          44

SMITH, SAMUEL (1602-1680)
                Stebbins, Albert Kellogg          53

SPAULDING, TIMOTHY (1676-1763)
                Reade, Philip          3

STANTON, THOMAS (1600-1677)
                Mason, William Lyman          17

STARK, AARON (1602-1685)
                Stark, Charles Gager          23
                Smith, William Stark          47

STARR, THOMAS (——1658)
                Starr, William James          21

WELLES, THOMAS (1598-1660)
          Strong, James Henry                              46
          Johnson, Francis Jewett                          49
          Jones, Charles Louis                             33

WETHERELL, DANIEL (1630-1719)
          Kennan, Thomas Lathrop                           52

WHEELOCK, ELEAZAR (1654-1731)
          Camp, Robert                                     25

WICOM, RICHARD (——1663)
          Johnson, Francis Jewett                          49

WILLARD, SIMON (1605-1676)
          Reade, Philip                                     3

WILLIAMS, CHARLES (1691-1769)
          Flint, Wyman Kneeland                             6

WILLIAMS, THOMAS (————)
          Flint, Wyman Kneeland                             6

WILSON, BENJAMIN (1747-1827)
          Smith, Benjamin Wilson                           42

WOLCOTT, ROGER (1678-1762)
          Strong, William Wolcott                           1

## INDEX TO NAMES OF MEMBERS

CPSIA information can be obtained
at www.ICGtesting.com
Printed in the USA
LVHW081600150422
716310LV00005B/270

9 781346 967555